CELESTE KANPURWALA

Bold Brave Goddess:

From Insecure Victim to Confident Survivor

This book is dedicated to those struggling to find their own bold brave goddess inside –
It's in there, I promise.

Introduction

Definition of "brave," from Oxford Languages:
"Ready to face and endure danger or pain; showing courage."

From Cheryl Strayed in *Brave Enough*:
"Bravery is acknowledging your fear and doing it anyway."

From Glennon Doyle in *Untamed*:
"To be brave is to forsake all others to be true to yourself."

From yours truly:
Being brave means being scared but sucking it up and kicking ass anyway!

I will never forget the Lady Gaga concert I attended with my mother.

Here I was with two of my sheroes in the same room – my incredibly resilient and takes-no-bullshit mom and the activist-multitalented-goddess Lady Gaga. As Gaga sat onstage being her brilliant badass self, she stated to the audience that if she were to be remembered for one thing in life, she would want it to be for her bravery. While I contemplated for many years what I would like to be remembered by, I eventually came to the realization that Lady Gaga has it right. We could be remembered for our kindness or our tenacity, but ultimately, courage is what really sets us apart from our fellow humans.

Nevertheless, it took a lot of convincing and self-encouragement for me to feel that I was worthy enough to write this book (and years for me to find the courage to publish it). Hell, I still have to tell myself this on a regular basis. Why is it that self-doubt and insecurities come so naturally to us, and it is easier for us to congratulate and cheer for others as they succeed? Many of us are so skeptical of ourselves.

It's time to change that. It's time to dig deep - to find that inner strength, that inner goddess, and tell ourselves that we are just as capable and just as worthy as anyone else on this planet of accomplishing our dreams. We are worthy of our own love and acceptance.

What I want you to see throughout my story and my life lessons is that despite all of the times I have been terrified to do things, when I have literally peed my pants or been shaking from head to toe, I somehow talked myself into advancing anyway because I knew that the end result was worth it. I know to just take a deep breath and put one foot in front of the other. As Cheryl Strayed puts it in *Brave Enough*, "Hello, fear. Thank you for being here. You're my indication that I'm doing what I need to do."

Throughout this book you will see quotes from various authors, speakers, artists, athletes, and influencers. My hope is that if you have not heard these quotes before, or even if you have, they can help inspire you along your journey. One of my very favorite quotes, of which I have the latter part tattooed on my arm, is yet again from the incredible Cheryl Strayed, who hiked the Pacific Coast Trail with no training and wrote about her experience:

"This is not the moment to wilt into the underbrush of your

insecurities. You've earned the right to grow."

May you continue to grow and to learn, to read and to live life to the fullest. **You are amazing.**

My goal in writing this book is to empower women and femme-identifying folx (and anyone on the gender spectrum who is brave enough to be part of this conversation) to be unapologetically themselves and to tell their stories, changing the narrative around mental health and self care.

Be Bold, Be Brave, because if you don't do something, who will? ™

Let's do this, loves!

I

My Story

"We are creatures who are born to transform pain into beauty." – Susan Cain, "How Sorrow and Longing Make Us Whole," Unlocking Us Podcast

1

Family History & My Childhood

"But monsters don't stay in boxes. They get out." – Dr. Sue Johnson, Hold Me Tight: Seven Conversations for a Lifetime of Love

This story begins before I was even born. My mother was married to a man (my father) who was deeply hurt by his family. All of their pain and drama affected his personality and the way that he treated people, especially my mother. My dad's oldest brother was tragically killed in a car accident at the age of 7, and my dad was born exactly one week later. Consequently, his second oldest brother, in his little 4-year-old brain, felt that his older brother had to die in order for his younger brother to be born. Talk about entering a fucked-up world! After their first-born was killed, my grandparents tried so hard to feel whole again, so they had baby after baby, trying to mend their broken hearts. They had 3 more babies after my dad was born, yet that intense feeling of loss was always there.

Later, I learned from paperwork and letters that my uncle sent me after my grandparents passed away that during this time and shortly thereafter, drama was unfolding in the Smith household. My grandpa was abusive to my grandma and their children, and my grandma tried leaving him multiple times from 1962 to 1966, when she finally left for good. Their children grew up knowing this very dysfunctional and broken household. Therefore, it came naturally to my dad to take his anger out on his wife and child, as that is exactly what he experienced. He didn't stop to assess why he acted that way. He let his anger control him - throwing things, punching walls, and playing Russian Roulette on himself in front of my mother while I was sleeping in the room next to them.

It's no wonder that my mother left my father when I was 3 years old. We moved in with my maternal grandparents for 4 ½ years, and they helped raise me, guiding me and instilling in me the principles that I hold dear. My mother and I grew close during those years, and I remember her promising me that we would eventually move in together, just the two of us.

However, when I was 8 years old, my mom remarried, giving me a new older stepbrother and soon after, a younger half-brother. This dramatic change, uprooting me from a suburban lifestyle with my grandparents and my mom's undivided attention, and then moving me to a farm in southwest Michigan with new family members...well, needless to say, I was not filled with joy at the turn of events. I was very jealous of my mom's new relationship, and I took it out on my new family members.

I had a hard time fitting into my new school system and making friends. It was clear that I was not one of the "popular" kids (which I am glad for now, but at the time it was very demeaning and frustrating). I lacked self-confidence. As time progressed, I morphed into an insecure teenager in junior high. In 8th grade, my English teacher and volleyball coach took advantage of my social status and my self-doubt, and he molested me both in his classroom after school and on the bus on the way to volleyball games. When my older brother, a high school senior at the time, found out that one of his classmates was sleeping with the same teacher, he also discovered my secret and convinced me to confess and tell our parents. I vividly remember sitting very awkwardly in a room with our head priest and having to explain to him the atrocities that this teacher committed. The teacher was forced to resign but no charges were pressed, since my family didn't want to make me sit through a trial. (He went on to teach at more schools. I don't know if he is still teaching, but I can only hope that karma is working its way toward him.)

Needless to say, this really fucked with my head. At 14 years old, as I was trying to negotiate my way through my emotions, puberty, and everything that comes with it, I was now also dealing with the repercussions of my teacher molesting me and me being the one who came forward and outed him. My feelings were quite ambivalent, not sure what to think – I was so ashamed and embarrassed because at the time *I actually liked it*. I struggled for years with this gross feeling. It wasn't until years later when I was sitting in therapy that I had a *Good Will Hunting* moment, filled with tears, repeating over and over again, "It's not my fault."

2

Anxiety Took Over

"Imagine if, in your hometown, four out of every ten broken legs went unaddressed, four out of every ten infections went untreated, four out of every ten heart attacks were ignored. We would say, 'That's unacceptable!' – and rightly so. It's just as unacceptable that mental illness goes unaddressed, untreated, and ignored." – Kamala Harris, *The Truths We Hold: An American Journey*

I HATE the feeling that anxiety gives me: my stomach in knots and the closing of my throat, like someone is slowly trying to squeeze my insides out of me via my mouth. This is not something I would want anyone to feel, except maybe the teacher who caused it in the first place. I speak about it so that others do not feel so alone. Anxiety is HELL and I am here to expose it for the monster that it is.

My anxiety began precisely in the midst of the molestation by my teacher, as I remember standing in front of his classroom and feeling nervous for the first time while speaking in front of a group. My throat tightened up and suddenly my body was covered in a cold clammy sweat. I had never experienced anything like it before. It was the beginning of anxiety for me, something I knew nothing about but would soon come to know all *too* well. Mental health issues are indeed hereditary, but they often surface from a specific trigger and our lives are shaken up.

Anxiety always reared its ugly head when I was forced to publicly speak, which is a necessity in many college classes (and in everyday life, for that matter). Because my Commercial Recreation & Tourism major involved numerous presentations, the anxiety resurfaced with a vengeance when I was a junior at Michigan State University, and I experienced a full-on panic attack for the first time. I was sitting in my dorm room, attempting to watch *Gilmore Girls*, when suddenly I couldn't breathe. I couldn't get out of my own head. I had no idea what was happening to me because I had never experienced anything like it. I didn't even have a word for the anxiety I was feeling. I knew about depression, but anxiety was not anything I had even heard of – which is precisely why I spend so much time talking about it now. At the time, I just kept trying to push the anxiety down deeper and ignore it, which only made it fester and grow.

In the summer of 2004, when I was in Mexico doing a study abroad, I had to give a speech at the end of my trip in front of my class *in Spanish*. I was fine speaking Spanish on a daily basis to my classmates, my host family, and the locals (I loved ordering food and drinks in the restaurants). However, when it came to speaking in front of a group, that anxious feeling that was sparked in my 8th grade teacher's class came rushing back to me. (*THANKS ASSHOLE!*) As a coping mechanism (because I still didn't know what the fuck to do about the god-awful

11

anxiety plaguing my poor body), I took up smoking again, after having quit two years prior, shortly after my maternal grandpa died from emphysema and pulmonary fibrosis after 30 years of smoking. As you'll soon read, addictions are ubiquitous amongst those of us who have experienced trauma.

Anxiety increased even more during my senior year in college when I took a course that required presentations virtually every single class. It was enough to make me question my self-confidence all over again. What I decided to do – the trick I decided to tell myself – only made things worse. I told myself that talking in front of this small group of people was just like talking to my friends. So guess what happened? I got nervous talking to people *all the fucking time.* *palm to forehead* I was even nervous talking to *my mom*! I was nervous by myself, and I was nervous talking to others. The only time I wasn't anxiety-ridden was while I was sleeping. It consumed my life. How I managed – I still don't know, but I can tell you that it took a crapload of bravery and endurance.

3

Alcoholism

"I drank to drown my sorrows, but the damned things learned how to swim." — Frida Kahlo, Source Unknown (But I'm going with it, because you know when people ask what famous person you would want to meet, alive or dead? My answer is Frida Kahlo.)

Now that we are done talking about my struggles with anxiety, we can get into my struggles with drinking. Yay! Because who doesn't want to talk about the shitty things they did while drinking? That sounds like a good time – said no one ever. *Sigh*. But here it goes.

Interestingly enough, I never was much of a drinker while I was in high school or college. It wasn't until I married my first husband and realized how incompatible we were and how unhappy I was that I took up drinking. (I should note that he is a great guy, we still stay in touch, and I am in no way blaming him for my actions.) I would go out with my friends and get wasted, then drive home. It wasn't until I nearly crashed my car and died that I realized I had a drinking and driving problem (I am convinced to this day that one of my guardian angels saved me that awful night). Did that stop me from continuing though? No.

After my first husband and I separated, I moved to Ann Arbor, MI. My friend Mark also lived in Ann Arbor, so we naturally started hanging out – tailgating, watching football games, going out to the clubs. We soon began dating and he proposed to me on March 1, 2011. At the time, he saw my drinking as an affliction of the young and foolish and believed that I was merely having fun.

However, it soon became apparent that I had a drinking problem, which only increased after we married, and even more so after my dad took his life. I began embarrassing my husband with my public intoxication. It became a constant argument between the two of us. Things only escalated once I started taking medication for my mental health, as it is a known no-no to mix alcohol and mental health drugs. Mark would point out to me that perhaps if I was feeling so depressed or anxious, wine was not the appropriate solution. I fought back, merely by attempting to hide my drinking. But Mark is no dummy.

Laura McKowen speaks about the tendency to drink to relieve our mental health issues and how this inevitably backfires in her book debut, *We Are the Luckiest: The Surprising Magic of a Sober Life.* In it, she states, "For so long, I thought alcohol had helped me relieve anxiety – that's what it promises, right? But somewhere along the line, I realized the equation was actually reversed: drinking alcohol was like pouring gasoline on my anxiety." I could relate only too well. Drinking to the point where my anxiety would linger just below the surface, cloaked in wine or vodka, choking and ready to spring back into life as soon as the booze wore off, became my coping mechanism.

After a few years, it came to the point where I would spend nights in the guest bedroom because I was too belligerently drunk to be around Mark. I thought I could fool him if I tried not to act "too drunk," but I wasn't fooling anyone. He began taking pictures of bottles of wine that I was secretly drinking, which I found on his phone. Even worse, our eldest son found a puke bucket next to my bed once or twice. This should have been enough to humiliate me. It wasn't.

My wakeup call came when Mark and the boys were gone on a weekend trip to Purdue (Mark's alma mater). I was going out with a friend for her birthday and promised Mark that I would only have a couple drinks. Yet, I took a Lyft into town.... The next thing I knew, I completely blacked out after taking shots and drinking an obscene amount of vodka, and I woke up the next day with one of the worst hangovers of my life. I could sense the anger mixed with fear in Mark's voice, keeping him up all night worrying while he was supposed to be on a fun boys trip. Suddenly I could no longer pretend that I was in control. That is when I realized I had a problem – it was my rock bottom.* I went to my first AA meeting 5 days later. My sobriety date is September 7, 2019.

Now that I am almost six years sober, and I know that I am never going back to drinking, I see how clear my thoughts are and how put together my life is. No longer do I look forward to nights out that fog up my mind. I don't go out to dinner anymore and order glass after glass of wine, or martini after martini. These things weren't serving me any more than they serve anyone using addictions to escape their problems. I wish that I could be someone who goes out and just orders one glass of wine to sip and enjoy with their dinner, but sadly I am not. And you know what? I am totally okay with not poisoning my body with the alcohol and the chemicals that are found in wine anyway (I highly recommend that you research the chemicals that are put into wine – you will be shocked).

*I would like to note that I, like Laura McKowen, am one of the lucky ones. Not everyone is able to move past their addictions. We lose way too many people on a daily basis to drugs and alcohol. Many folks go through much worse than I did before hitting their rock bottom. I can only speak for myself and hope that it helps others who are struggling.

4

Hearing Loss

"The disempowerment that comes with not being able to hear is incomparable." – Jen Pastiloff, *On Being Human*

One lonely afternoon, I found myself in a daze, with a beautiful melody from Matchbox Twenty blaring in my ears, succumbing to the fact that my hearing loss was getting worse. I was diagnosed with hearing loss several years ago, something I already knew but didn't want to admit. It wasn't until my mom came over and asked me why I had subtitles on the TV, to which I indignantly replied, "Because I can't hear that well." This was news to her. In typical mom fashion, she immediately ordered me to go to the doctor. The doctor told me that my hearing loss is equivalent to someone who worked in a loud factory for 10 years. He asked me if I did; I said no. Two things come to mind - 1. My constant ear infections as a kid, including once on Christmas Eve when my poor mom had to deal with my painful moaning in the middle of the night, and 2. My inherited obsession (thanks Dad) with loud music. I used to blast my music in my teenage angst, drowning out the world with Nirvana and Garbage.

The doctor ordered a series of tests to see if I have Meniere's Disease, something for which there is no cure and no known cause either. According to Mayo Clinic, "Symptoms include a spinning sensation (vertigo), hearing loss, ear ringing (tinnitus), and ear pressure. The vertigo may cause severe nausea and imbalance. Hearing loss may become permanent."

Yep, I had/have all of these symptoms. The test, however, was inconclusive. One section of it pointed toward yes, the other no. Either way, the hearing loss is obvious. It's frustrating having to tell my kids that Mommy can't hear them.

Hearing loss is a sneaky bitch. I was in denial for so long. I thought people just mumbled more and more. I didn't want to admit it might be MY issue. Yet when the doctor told me to cut back on my coffee intake, my knee jerk reaction was to drink MORE coffee (which has only gotten worse as I become more of a coffee snob with each passing day). Sigh. Defiant feisty Celeste. Sometimes she is a badass; other times she is a *pain* in the ass.

Whatever caused my hearing loss, I know it's here to stay. I might as well get used to asking people to repeat themselves. I'm much more candid now about my condition. It seems less off-putting I suppose than asking "what?!" over and over again.

Thank the goddess (credit to Audre Lorde for this idiom) for subtitles!

5

Love, Marriage & Divorce

"People always fall in love with the most perfect aspects of each other's personalities. Who wouldn't? Anybody can love the most wonderful parts of another person. But that's not the clever trick. The really clever trick is this: Can you accept the flaws? Can you look at your partner's faults honestly and say, 'I can work around that. I can make something out of it.'? Because the good stuff is always going to be there, and it's always going to pretty and sparkly, but the crap underneath can ruin you." – Elizabeth Gilbert, *Committed: A Love Story*

So, let's talk about my failed first marriage. I am just loads of fun, aren't I? Talking about abuse, molestation, alcohol, divorce.... The point is, I want you to understand where I came from to get to where I am today. I had to suffer so much pain before I could crawl my way out of the darkness and get to the beautiful place that I am in today. Do I still have hard days? Absolutely. But because I know what it's like to be in such a low, horrible place, I know what I am capable of – I know that I am capable of getting myself to a better place. I know that I can withstand the storm of whatever it is I might be going through.

My first husband is an amazing man. We were college sweethearts. He treated me well. We were just total opposites, and eventually it tore us apart. We tried marriage therapy. It was miserable and uncomfortable. Because I am outgoing and have a lot to say, I would sit there and ramble on and on while husband #1 sat silently. He was the type who needed a day to respond. It drove me nuts! I would sometimes spout off to him about something, and he wouldn't have a response, so I would think, "Ha, I knew I was right!" The next day, however, he would come back with a list of prepared points. It pissed me off!

I made the decision to end our marriage. (I left him the day he had just picked up a chainsaw from some creeper on Craigslist, which I now find hilarious.) While it was my decision, it was nonetheless the most difficult thing I have ever done. I knew that I was doing the right thing, but it hurt me to my core. I spent many days and nights sobbing in my new lonely apartment. I sought solace with drunken nights at the bar and one-night stands. During this time, I dated a handful of losers (one of them later went to jail for statutory rape, so that just goes to show the level of self-respect I had for myself during this time).

Finally, after Mark and I were friends for months, and he followed my drunken sloppy shameful escapades, he somehow fell in love with me. Well, let's be honest, he fell in love with my dog first. My sweet, goofy, handsome golden retriever named Rocky whom I lovingly called RockStar. Mark told me I could only come over to his condo if Rocky was coming with me. That worked for me! He quickly had my heart. The first time I told him that I loved him was because of the way he loved on my

RockStar. We fell for each other hard and fast. I knew quickly that he was the one for me, but I made him wait to marry me since I was just coming from a failed marriage. I had sworn that I wouldn't marry again for a while, and if I did, I would elope.

That plan didn't pan out, considering I was marrying a 36-year-old man whose enormous family had been waiting for him to marry (this is his first and only marriage), and they rightfully wanted to celebrate in a big way! Not only did we have a Nikah (Muslim ceremony); complete with the "traditional" separation of men and women into two different rooms, which upset my hippie feminist mom so much that she took the ceremony as an opportunity to get her afternoon nap in; we also had a religious reception months later before finally having our own American ceremony and reception. Our American ceremony was the quickest ceremony that our wedding coordinator at the hotel had ever seen, as she made the mistake of trying to eat dinner during it, but it was over and done in 5 minutes!

Marrying Mark was one of the smartest decisions I have ever made to this day. We celebrated our 10 year anniversary in October 2021 by renewing our vows on the beautiful island of Bora Bora in the South Pacific. While I could write a book about our marriage, I will merely state that Mark and I have grown together and encouraged each other to be our absolute best selves. We have supported one another through life changes, losses, and incredible successes. He is the ultimate soulmate, accepting me for who I am and allowing me to morph into the bold brave goddess that I was called to be.

6

My Dad's Death & PTSD

"When someone you love dies, especially if your relationship wasn't ideal, there is a second death you must accept. There's the death of the person and the death of all the hopes you had for them." – Kory M. Shrum, *Who Killed my Mother?*

My relationship with my dad was tumultuous, seasonal, and very much controlled by his mental health issues. While I prefer to remember the good times, all too often I find myself wincing as I am instantaneously transported back in time to days when he refused to talk to me for some random stupid thing that I said or did. The manipulation and gaslighting left scars on my soul.

Perhaps the biggest disappointment that my father inflicted on me is that he did not attend my wedding to the love of my life. This hurts even typing it out. I asked him the moment that Mark and I got engaged if he would walk me down the aisle, to which he replied that he couldn't commit to doing so because he didn't know how he would feel. My mom had walked me down the aisle at my first wedding, so this time I wanted to give my dad the opportunity to do so. I understood that his noncommittal answer was due to his lifelong depression, so instead I asked my step-dad to do it. He didn't disappoint. Not only did he walk me down the aisle, but he told me to walk slowly "so that everyone could bask in my beauty." (He also helped corral about 100 of Mark's loud family members into the room to sit down for the ceremony, which was impressive.)

I called my dad weeks before our wedding to ask if he would be attending, and he never bothered to call me back. I was so distraught that I laid in bed sobbing, telling Mark that I wished that he would just die so I wouldn't worry about him so much (which caused extreme guilt and remorse when he took his own life 2.5 years later). Hell, I didn't know if he was having a medical emergency or just not returning my calls! When I called him the day of my wedding to ask if he would be coming, he finally admitted that he was not. This is NOT the ideal thing for a bride to hear on her wedding day while attempting to get ready and not smear her makeup.

Can I just pause here and say, *FUCK*!!! The emotions that stir up in me are painful. I find myself stopping to stare blankly into space. Shit, it was easier to tell my own stories of failure and addiction than it is to talk of my dad's depression and suicide. I have learned through my speeches with Moms Demand Action (don't worry, I'll get into that soon) to be kind and gentle to myself after talking about my dad, because the emotions that it brings out in me are absolutely exhausting.

When I gave birth to my firstborn, my dad called me in the hospital to congratulate me on becoming a mom. This was nearly 2 years after my wedding, and I hadn't spoken to him much since then. I was still bitter that he abandoned me on my wedding day. He did come to our Nikah (which in his mind was the important ceremony because he was very spiritual and respected all religions), but only because I picked him up and took him back home. This would have been difficult for me to do during our larger American wedding with hundreds of people coming from out of town. Yet my dad somehow managed to make me feel guilty for not also driving him back and forth for that (he hadn't driven his truck in years, so it was essentially non-functional in his driveway). He had a way of making me feel guilty nearly every time I talked to him. This is another form of abuse, also known as mind-fuckery, manipulation, and gaslighting at its finest. I dated a few guys who did this to me as well, as it is what I grew up with and knew. I said I would never be in those relationships, but unfortunately our bodies do crazy things that our minds don't control. (Here I would recommend the book, *The Body Keeps the Score* by the incredible Dr. Bessel van der Kolk to understand what I am talking about.) Luckily I was smart enough not to marry any of these mind-fuckers. Both of the men I married are straight-forward, good men.

The scars of guilt that my dad cursed me with still resurface frequently. As time passes, the pain lessens, but it is still there, and it will likely never go away. *I don't think it is supposed to.* I think the pain is there to remind me of the emotional abuse that I endured. The pain is there to remind me that even though I am a survivor of suicide, and it hurts that my dad is gone, and it still feels surreal to say that my dad took his life, the truth of the matter is that the pain he caused me in life was nearly as difficult as the pain that he is now causing me in death. In fact, my husband and I were discussing the matter of eliminating him from my life when he decided to kill himself the day after my birthday on April 9, 2014. Mark and I had paid for two months of his rent, and when he ran out of money, he took his life.

The PTSD that I still suffer from walking across the threshold in his apartment and having to step across a barren floor, where the carpet had been ripped out and the floorboards were painted a glossy white to cover up the bloodstains, still haunts me. When my mom handed me my dad's precious Longchamp wallet (which evoked memories of shopping for it in Switzerland together two decades prior), I lost it. Fortunately, my sweet husband had secured an outside company to come in and help get rid of everything in his apartment, because I was pretty useless in my grief. One thing that I did do was sit down at his computer and look at his e-mails. He had e-mailed me on my birthday, the day before he killed himself, to tell me how much he loved me and always will. I still have that e-mail. The guilt I felt in not responding immediately to his e-mail was lessened when I saw all of my dad's unread e-mails, including one from a local music store that he had e-mailed about selling his music equipment to so that he could make more money to live on. I think the moment he e-mailed the music store, he realized that he couldn't live without his precious music (I mean, who would want to?), so he just sat around and waited to kill himself. According to my mother, he wouldn't have been cruel enough to kill himself on my birthday, so he did it the day after. I just rolled my eyes at that, because really, what's one day?

While my birthdays have never been the same, I have worked hard to reclaim my joy and not let my dad take away the fun of celebrating my special day. He has been gone for over a decade now, and I know that he would ultimately want me to be happy. I heard it in his voice when he called me shortly before he died; he said to me that he could hear how happy I sounded, and that in turn made him happy.

7

Motherhood & Moms Demand Action

"You may not feel like a badass if your voice and hands are shaking or your knees are knocking, but you absolutely are." – Shannon Watts, *Fight Like a Mother: How a Grassroots Movement Took on the Gun Lobby and Why Women Will Change the World*

On December 12, 2012, I found out that I was going to be a mom. I will never forget that special feeling, as my husband and I had been trying for about 6 months to conceive (which isn't too bad I know, and I am forever grateful that we were able to conceive naturally). Because we had been trying for several months and I had already taken a handful of pregnancy tests, it was becoming habit for me to pee on a stick. So when I suspected I might be pregnant yet again, which happened a few times over those months, I stopped at a CVS on my way to the mall to do some holiday shopping, and I took the test in the public bathroom stall while Frosty the Snowman played joyfully overhead. Much to my delight, I was finally pregnant! My mom and husband were the first to know, followed by my beloved grandmother, who I happened to be taking out to dinner and staying with that night.

I spent the next day and a half in a state of euphoria – until I came home for lunch from my hotel sales job on Friday, December 14, turned on our little kitchen TV, and saw to my horror that a bunch of first graders and educators were murdered in their school in Newtown, CT. This put me in a constant state of panic and anxiety, wondering *how in the fuck* I could bring a child into this hell that we were living in where little children could be murdered in their classrooms. I was scared I might lose my baby due to my anxiety and fear.

Fortunately, I did not lose my sweet child, and he is now a thriving boy who likes to torment his brother. Many other families in the meantime lost their children, all of varying ages, due to gun violence. For the 3 years following the Sandy Hook massacre, every time that a mass shooting occurred and was splattered all over the news, I would take to social media and rant. I would blog. I would spout off in my anger and my fear, and I would spend the following weeks in a state of panic yet again. The cycle would continue.

Finally, after 3 years of me just talking and writing, I committed to doing something tangible. I thought I would start a change.org petition, but instead my husband found something even better for me. He found Everytown for Gun Safety, which led me to my local Moms Demand Action for Gun Sense in America meeting. Now here is where I will give you time to research Moms Demand Action for yourself. This is not for me to tell you what the organization is about, as our founder, Shannon Watts, does a great job of that in her own book (which I highly recommend), *Fight Like a Mother*.

My first Moms Demand Action meeting found me writing care cards for survivors of a shooting in Kalamazoo, a southwestern city in Michigan where I spent a decent amount of time as a child, as my mother worked there for 12 years. I would often accompany her to her job at Social Security when she had to work overtime on Saturdays, taking naps and reading in her car while she worked, and afterward we would go out for lunch and shop. This shooting that killed 6 people in a town I was so familiar with just tore me up inside. It really hit close to home, literally.

While decorating my care cards and writing the most sincere, loving messages I could think of for these unfortunate souls, I happened to mention to the woman sitting across from me, who was the founder of our Michigan Moms Demand Action chapter, that my dad took his life with his shotgun. She stopped what she was doing to look me square in the eye, and she told me that I am a survivor of gun violence. *What?? ME?!* I thought survivors of gun violence were only people who had been shot or people who survived these horrific mass shootings that you saw in the media. I thought survivors of gun violence were war veterans, police officers, gang members or people who happened to be somewhere when a crazed person unleashed horror with a gun.

Oh, how little did I know. Not only did I not realize my own status as a survivor of gun violence, but I had no idea how truly ubiquitous gun violence is in this country (and how privileged I am to first experience gun violence in my thirties). I didn't know about the daily victims and survivors of suicide, homicide, domestic violence, and unintentional shootings – currently over 100 people die in this country each day from a gun. I could go on and on about all of the depressing statistics and facts that I have learned since joining Moms Demand Action, but again I will leave it to you to do your own research. I suggest our parent website, http://everystat.org.

After attending one meeting, *I knew I had found my passion and my people.*

8

Survivor Life with Moms Demand Action and Everytown for Gun Safety

"Nobody's tears are heavier than the other. Who wants to compete with grief?" – Julvonnia McDowell, "Black-on-Black Violence," *It's the Miami Knight Show – Grief Talk* Podcast

Every year, Moms Demand Action hosts an event in June called National Gun Violence Awareness Day, or Wear Orange. Every year we honor the victims and survivors of gun violence in one weekend, and we wear orange, for it is the color that hunters wear to protect themselves from other hunters with guns in the woods. After I had been involved with Moms Demand Action for a little over a year, the planning committee for the Wear Orange event asked me to speak. I thought about it for approximately 2 seconds and said no, stating that I didn't feel comfortable speaking in front of a group AND my dad's death was still too fresh for me (3 years at that point). However, I posed like a diva for pictures, showing my poignant survivor face at the event.

That same year, about 2 months later, I attended my first Moms Demand Action annual conference, where I met Frederick Wright. Fred and his wife MJ's son, Jerry, was murdered at the Pulse Nightclub shooting. Meeting Fred and seeing how he was already part of this organization after losing his son just over a year prior was a pivotal point for me. I looked down at his nametag and saw that his title was Survivor Fellow. I asked him what that meant, and he explained that it was a national program for survivors. Fred and I cried and hugged, and we took a picture together, especially since I fortuitously had worn my rainbow Disarm Hate t-shirt that day (which our organization had made in response to the Pulse Nightclub shooting).

After returning home and still reeling from all of the survivor stories that I had heard at the conference, I knew that something big was in store for me. This Survivor Fellow role kept ringing in my mind, and I asked my regional manager about it. She assured me that she would send me the application once the role was open for the following year. *Application?* Wow. Since I was so accustomed to my Moms Demand Action volunteer role that I was thrust into, I was a bit intimidated that I had to apply.

I knew I had it in me though.

When the application was sent to me, I confidently completed it (well, that's a lie; I was actually sick with a fever when I completed it, but I was told that it was nonetheless impressive). When it was time for my interview, I researched the person who would be interviewing me and was actually watching her impressively testify to legislators on YouTube when she called me. This helped open up our conversation, and she asked me questions that I had already prepared myself for, such as how I would handle audience members who were heckling me while I was speaking to them.

Here I suppose I should further explain what it means to be a Survivor Fellow. This role is meant to give voice to all survivors of gun violence throughout the country, where we tell our stories in front of audiences throughout the year. This could be at meetings, rallies, local clubs; in front of legislators, testifying in the state House or Senate; or just giving casual talks in front of friends. It REQUIRES us to tell our story though. It requires us to do that uncomfortable thing that just months prior I was too scared to do – the thing that many of my fellow humans are so scared to do – public speaking!

Suddenly I would have to ditch all of my preconceptions about public speaking and my anxiety about it that was triggered by that asshole teacher that you read about earlier. Something in me, though, knew that I was born to play this role. **I felt it in my bones that this was going to become my path.** The interview went very well, but I was told that the organization would not be able to accept everyone who applied into the program. I told myself that if it were meant to be, then it would be.

How elated I was when I received the phone call from the same amazing woman who interviewed me, to tell me that I was accepted into the program! I would be going to Washington D.C. to train with everyone else who was accepted into the program. I told my supportive group of mama friends (which you will read about soon), and they were happy right along with me.

Then, on February 14, 2018, merely about a week after finding out that I was now becoming an Everytown for Gun Safety Survivor Fellow, the tragic Parkland shooting happened in Florida while my family was also in Florida for our mid-winter break at Disney World. We were in line waiting to see Princess Jasmine and Prince Ali when I happened to glance at Mark's phone to see a text from my mother that said something like, "I am so glad you are with Celeste right now...." My immediate thought was, *FUCK – another shooting*. I was right. My family knows me all too well.

That night, we watched MSNBC and CNN coverage from our hotel room. On the news, I saw someone who would soon become my friend and mentor, Richard Martinez, whose son Christopher was murdered in the Isla Vista shooting the same year that my dad was killed. I watched as he told the reporters that these students in Florida knew more about gun drills than legislators. Richard had given me his son's honorary wristband to wear when I met him at the conference the year before, with his signature tagline NOT ONE MORE. I soaked in every word that Richard told the reporters.

Within the next month, I found myself planning and speaking at the Ann Arbor March for Our Lives, which was a crowd of approximately 5000 people. My formal training to become a Survivor Fellow wasn't scheduled until the following month. I looked out at the crowd of people and literally peed my pants before getting onstage to speak. Nevertheless, **I crushed my speech.**

For someone who was a nervous wreck speaking in front of a group of only 10 people, this was a huge accomplishment for me! I had written my speech weeks before, also having delivered it to a local group of students who participated in a walk-out in early March. I practiced my speech every single day because I wanted it to be powerful. I borrowed what Richard said about students knowing more about gun drills than legislators, and I also expounded upon something that one of the student survivors (possibly Delaney Tarr) said on national TV – she demanded that adults stop telling them how brave they are. I addressed the students and told them that they *know* that they are brave and that they need to **keep going** (a signature Moms Demand Action tagline). I told them that

33

our Moms Demand Action membership had surpassed the NRA membership in our short, at the time, 5-year existence. I told my survivor story in front of this huge crowd, and I didn't shed a tear (because I was too nervous)! The cheers and the high that the audience gave me lasted for weeks.

I was so proud of myself.

9

Addressing my Mental Health

"It is far braver, not to mention healthier, to dive into our difficult emotions as they arise than to suppress or ignore them." - Ellen Vora, *The Anatomy of Anxiety: Understanding and Overcoming the Body's Fear Response*

In spite of my bravery and pride, something had happened to me once I learned that I was a survivor of gun violence. I took on the role completely. It became the main part of who I was. At parties, with friends and strangers, I constantly spoke of my role as a survivor and discussed my dad's suicide. It was, quite frankly, depressing. Every time that a new mass shooting made the news, more rage and anxiety surfaced. After the Las Vegas concert shooting occurred in October 2017, I hit a new low. Depression sank in and I began having suicidal ideations. I expressed this to Mark at the time, but since he had never suffered from mental health conditions, he didn't know how to respond or help me. I didn't know how to help myself.

In July 2018, our family vacationed in Aruba with more of Mark's family members. It was a vacation that I couldn't wait to go on, because Mark, being the sweet husband and amazing gift-giver that he is, bought me two yoga classes at Island Yoga. He knew that I had been following the owner, Rachel Brathen, for some time, listening to and feeling inspired by her podcasts. For Mother's Day that year, he bought me her book, *Yoga Girl*, along with these two classes, one of which was a water class taught on paddle boards in the ocean.

Unfortunately, the prospect of relaxing in Aruba and taking these incredible yoga classes was not enough to calm my anxiety. I found myself wanting to crawl out of my own skin and just *die* while I was on the airplane with my family heading down to paradise. Awful is an understatement for the way I was feeling, and I wouldn't wish it on my worst enemy.

Somehow I made it through the plane ride, and as soon as we landed and had dinner on our first night, I immediately began drowning my anxiety in wine. A couple of days later, after taking my first class at Island Yoga, I heard the teacher talking with other students about the reiki that she performs. *What was this reiki?* I approached her and asked her what purpose it serves. It turns out that it serves the exact purpose I was looking for – to help ease anxiety and clear my body & mind from all of my negative thoughts. I quickly booked my appointment to follow my paddleboard yoga class two days later.

To say I was apprehensive is an understatement! I walked into the yoga studio nervous to tell my story and express my fears. Nevertheless, I did it. The amount of love and understanding I received from my reiki master, Stephanie Moore, touched me so deeply. I told her of my dad's suicide, and she responded by saying that he asked me for forgiveness. I informed her that I already forgave him for what he did, but she told me that him asking is a different story. *Talk about powerful!*

After ridding myself of the negative thoughts, Stephanie proceeded to rid me of my negative energy too, while I laid silently on the massage bed. She ran her hands above my body, and I could feel her powerful positive energy coursing its way through me. After she was done and I opened my eyes, she asked me if I had a recurring thought throughout the process. I told her my thought was, "Love, Not Fear." She took a deep breath and said that happened to be one of her mantras and hashtags on social media. It has also become mine, and I now have it tattooed on my right foot in my mother's beautiful cursive handwriting.

While the reiki helped me temporarily, unfortunately it did not rid my body of the anxiety. It quickly returned after coming home, and I continued to suffer off and on with crippling anxiety and depression for the next several months. It wasn't until I finally decided to take medication that I was able to keep my thoughts under control and stop constantly doubting myself. The difference is staggering when I think about it. The feelings of helplessness and fear are still fresh in my brain.

10

Therapy, Medication, & Finally Taking Control

"For there is always light,

If only we're brave enough to see it,

If only we're brave enough to be it." – Amanda Gorman, *The Hill We Climb*

Fortunately, my mother recognized the signs of my mental health struggles after my sexual assault and throughout my father's emotional abuse, and she got me the help that I needed. Without her persistence, I have no idea where I would be today. She encouraged me as I explored a few different therapists before finding one that finally suited me, something that I have had to do a few times as I continue this lifelong journey of therapy work. There is no pride here when it comes to my mental health, and I will *always* advocate for doing whatever you need to help you on your journey (as long as it is truly helping, not harming).

I fought the idea of taking medication for years, taking pride in the fact that I wasn't "altering my brain." I was totally in control of my thoughts! HA! **The reality of it was that I was NOT in control.** My emotions were constantly in turmoil. I felt things *so hard, so raw, so real.* I felt the extreme highs and the extreme lows, and meanwhile my brain was flitting all over the place. I talked fast, I thought fast; hell, half the time, my mouth couldn't even keep up with my brain, and I slurred or stumbled over my words. This would only make my anxiety worse.

It wasn't my own self-love and self-worth that made me decide to start taking an anti-anxiety medication, but my love for my husband and my children, that inspired me to finally swallow my pride and take medication. I also had to try a few before I found the right fit for me. Lexapro caused suicidal ideations – oh, the irony! While I can be light-hearted about it now, it was not comical at the time, and it certainly is serious. If you are ever on a medication and start to notice dark thoughts (or if you notice dark thoughts *ever* really), please call your doctor and seek help. Thankfully I recognized the symptoms quickly and called my doctor to switch my medication.

The medication that I was then put on is Prozac, which I took for over two years, until the vivid dreams they caused got the best of me. For two whole years though, that medication was my miracle drug that kept me sane and balanced all of the chemicals in my brain, because that is all mental health issues are – chemical imbalances! (It's often compared to breaking a leg, right? If you had a broken leg, you would go to the doctor! Why not fix the most important thing – your brain?!)

After being on Prozac for 4 months, I had my annual physical with my doctor, and I mentioned to her that I was unable to fully orgasm on Prozac. (They don't tell you this little-known fact when they are prescribing these medications, but yes, sexual side effects are the number one side effect.) I told her that I heard good things about Wellbutrin, and she immediately put me on it, without much conversation. I did express my concern that Wellbutrin is known to sometimes increase anxiety, which is a much bigger problem for me than depression. However, I thought, "let me just try to this so that I can feel a full orgasm again" (since it had been **months**). Well, shit!! If I had known the severe anxiety and the panic attack that would ensue while I was vacationing with some of my dearest friends a week later, I would have said FUCK THAT NOISE. Not to mention the insomnia, irritation, cramping, and loss of appetite...Needless to say, I switched back to the Prozac faster than my eldest son can devour a bowl of ice cream!

After putting up with the vivid dreams that Prozac is also known for but rarely discussed, I finally had enough and was brave enough to try one more drug. That drug is Zoloft, which I am now taking as of this writing. I had to quickly increase my dose though, due to the differences between Prozac and Zoloft, and the anxiety that returned on a lower dose of Zoloft. Every single mental health medication has caused weird dreams. Oh, the joys of side effects! I always tell myself that it's better than the alternative. Better to have weird dreams and a decreased libido than to feel anxious 24/7.

This is a large portion of my story for a reason. My point is this: anxiety, depression, bipolar disorder, schizophrenia, etc. – they are ALL mental health conditions that MUST be treated if you want to function properly in this world and enjoy life for all its worth. After all, there is only one short life that we have – don't you want to be able to live it to its fullest while you are here?

You must be your biggest advocate!

II

My Community

"One stranger who understands your experience exactly will do for you what hundreds of close friends and family who don't understand cannot." – Laura McKowen, We Are the Luckiest

11

The LGBTQ Community & My Bisexuality

"Labels are for packages, not sexuality." - Rebel Wilson, *Rebel Rising: A Memoir*

When I was in fourth grade, I dreamt that I fell asleep in bed next to a boy classmate of mine and that I woke up next to a girl classmate of mine (completely non-sexual). I had a crush on the boy, but I questioned why in the world this girl was in my bed...what did it mean? Was I attracted to girls?! I pushed that thought deep down and didn't revisit it until high school, when I finally admitted to myself that I was/am attracted to women. I told my mom about it, and she insisted that it was just a phase I was going through. Ha! I must note here that my mom is extremely accepting of the queer community, and I think she truly thought it was just temporary or exploratory for me. I knew differently though.

When I entered college at Michigan State University, I immediately joined one of the queer support groups and made lifelong friendships. I took on a leadership role within the organization, and I remember sitting there in our closeknit circle, stating how I wanted to be so bold as to introduce myself to everyone I met as, "Hi, my name is Celeste, and I'm bisexual." I never did get that brave, but it definitely made for great conversation with those friends!

I marched in a couple of queer parades on campus, and I was interviewed for a local TV station after one of them. I was so ecstatic to see myself on TV that I even recorded it (and this was back when you had to set your recording on a videotape, for those who are old enough to remember). Being involved in queer advocacy exposed me to social injustices. I learned what it was like to be discriminated against, both by the gay community and the heterosexual community, who can sometimes find it hard to comprehend what it's like to be attracted to both/all sexes and/or genders. I also learned how to accept people that I didn't understand at the time – the transgender community. I stumbled over my pronouns when a friend of mine transitioned. It inspired me to learn more, research more, and LISTEN more to other people's perspectives and stories.

Being a part of the queer activist group at MSU was so critical for my growth. It taught me acceptance and understanding. It also set me up for speaking up for human rights, and it got the ball rolling in my lifelong pursuit of social justice.

12

Supportive Mom/Caregiver Groups

"Very few things in life will get you further than a loyal group of women who are supportive of you because you are supportive of them." – Lydia Fenet, *The Most Powerful Woman in the Room is You*

While motherhood is indeed my favorite job that I have ever had, most moms would agree with me that it is indeed the hardest one. A supportive group that has completely changed my outlook on life is a group of mothers, which was founded by the incredibly talented, kind, generous, beautiful Erica Stoebick. Little did I know going into this group that my life was about to be made exponentially better. Little did I know that this small group of women was going to teach me so much about myself, the way I treated people, the way I mothered my children, and my outlook on life in general.

Erica saw a need for support in motherhood, so she began creating Facebook groups to provide exactly that. The only stipulations were that you had to be a soon-to-be mama or already have at least one child, and you had to be open-minded.

The group was formed only by word of mouth, and I was so lucky to be invited into the group by one of my grandma's caretakers who has a little boy of her own.

When I was invited into the group, there was another mother who had recently posted about her child's seizures. My friend tagged me in the post and asked me if I could comment with my experience. I went in with my typical know-it-all attitude, saying exactly what I went through with my own son's seizures, assuming that my answers would be the solution that this mama was seeking. She responded by saying something to the effect of, "Hmmm, OK, thanks."

Wait, what? What just happened? Wasn't I invited into this group for my invaluable knowledge and experience? Wasn't I needed? I went on to internally pout and think that maybe I should have just stayed involved in my own local mom group. In fact, I came very close to exiting the group, but something made me stay.

Over the next few months, I noticed that this group was constantly posting pictures and updates about their little ones, especially on what they called, "Tot Tuesdays." After a while, I was inspired to join in and share pictures too; I wanted to be part of their fun! The next thing I knew, I would find myself staying up late at night looking through and reacting to and/or commenting on everyone else's pictures!

Next, we began to have get-togethers, as many of our members lived in metro-Detroit, not much more than an hour from where I live in Ann Arbor. As I got more involved, I was struck by how welcoming and non-judgmental these moms were. Everyone's parenting style and life choices were treated with love and respect. It was so refreshing compared to the constant online bullying and judgement being tossed all over the damn Internet.

After many posts, updates and articles from Erica and the other moms, I began noticing a shift in my own approach to motherhood and the way that I looked at others. No longer was I questioning why a mom chose to breastfeed or not (or any other decisions that she made for her child(ren) or family), because I knew that no matter what, the babies were getting the nourishment and love they needed. No longer did I criticize my body type as much in the mirror, because our group was full of different shapes and sizes, and we embraced and celebrated them all. No longer did I feel so much guilt for not being the "perfect" mom, because I know from seeing everyone else's mommy mishaps that everyone is just trying their damn best. This mindset is so liberating!

I attribute much of my humanity and kindness to Erica and my fellow moms in this special group. **I would not be where I am today without them.**

13

Working Out & Running

"I'm not super interested in exploring the easy route." – Des Linden, on her Instagram account, @des_linden

My supportive, motivational husband would often say to me as we began dating that he was "heading to the gym." I would sit in my apartment in front of my computer, checking Facebook, talking about how I didn't have time to work out. *What?!* I didn't have kids or other responsibilities outside of work, other than my dog. What did I have to do that was so important as to neglect my body?

Finally, Mark convinced me to try his gym by enticing me with a hip hop class led by an engaging and energetic man named Rodney. I was so intrigued! While I had a history of dancing, I was quickly reminded that it was not my forte. There was a reason that I hadn't been part of a dancing group since elementary school, when I was forced to wear those ridiculously frilly outfits and makeup fit for a clown! (Oh, how I love looking at the pictures though.) While I became a hip hop class regular, I cringed every time I was called on to demonstrate the dance we were working on in front of the class.

The same went for an incredible Zumba class led by a beautiful woman named Hanife. While it was fun and definitely cultivated some amazing friendships, I had to find something that I was better at and that didn't embarrass me. I felt like a stomping elephant traveling across the room amongst a herd of prancing deer. To this day, when I participate in dance-themed workouts, I second-guess every single move and wish I were just running on my own.

A kickboxing class that I decided to try next made me feel powerful. I was able to take out my aggression from work during class. Any drama I was carrying with me got released with punches and kicks. It was awesome! Soon I was taking barre classes, weight classes, and whole-body workout classes.

It was when we switched to a gym with an indoor track that I decided to take up running, which I had always hated. However, a year prior, when Mark and I participated in the Detroit Susan G. Komen Race for the Cure, I made myself slowly jog those 3.1 miles in memory of my dear friend Carrie Noble, who passed away in 2008 from breast cancer that metastasized to her lungs and brain. She was only 34 years old with two small children. She and I worked together for a hotel in Dearborn, MI, and I will always remember her kind heart, her generosity, her strength, and her beautiful smile.

After slogging (that's a slow jog for those who don't know) that first 5K, I abruptly decided the following year, one month before the annual Susan G. Komen race, to start practicing. I wanted to be able to keep up with my husband who was my fiancé then. Not only did I keep up with him, but afterward when I found myself panting and out of breath, I experienced my first runner's high. I had caught the runner's bug! Soon I began running longer distances and quickly increased from 5K to 10K, then onto a half marathon. Finally in 2015, between the births of our two children, I was able to complete my one and only marathon with the help of my running buddies Brian and Ray, as well as the assistance of my running coach Ryan Knapp. (Major props to hubby for purchasing that coaching package for me – I wouldn't have done it without that kick in the arse!)

I started attending Boot Camp classes at our gym, which I still love, involving running and other cardio exercises (such as the dreaded burpees...I love you Sara, Lisa, and Andrea if any of you are reading this) and weight exercises. I enjoy moving my body in this way and have learned that for my personality type and my anxiety management, working out is a necessity. It helps relieve the tension and stress. It is one of my many forms of self care.

Running brings me clarity. It gives me space to think. Sometimes I use it for inspiration, listening to a podcast while pumping my legs, or simply coming up with a motivational Live, post, or blog to deliver or write down when I am done. Sometimes I just like to tune the world out and listen to music that keeps me going. It's kind of like life – we all have our own ways of getting through and dealing. **You have to find what works for you.**

*After the initial publication of this book, I had to re-evaluate everything after a bad fall in my kitchen. I wasn't even doing anything cool - just rushing to get our puppy Lily something to chew on that wasn't our property...when one of my slippers, that I was wearing mind you, got tripped up on the other one... and I landed hard and fast on both knees. One knee bruised and recovered. The other one now has barely any cartilage to show for itself. Soooo, I am back to dancing instead of running. I still look like an ungraceful animal of some kind, but I have learned to embrace it - while having fun in the process!

14

Yoga

"The poses we practice are not the destination, but the path."
– Rachel Brathen, *Yoga Girl*

I remember taking my first yoga class with a friend who dragged me to it while I was in college. I tried showing off, thinking I was so flexible, which was laughable. My next yoga experience took place during my senior-year internship on the island of St. John, Virgin Islands, volunteering at an eco-tourist campground called Maho Bay Camps (which, sadly, does not exist anymore). Practicing yoga in an elevated pavilion while surrounded by the aqua-colored Caribbean Sea, which resembled a postcard every day, hooked me.

I returned from St. John and began practicing using home DVDs and trying to will myself into being more flexible each time. I remember struggling with warrior poses and simple forward folds. Practicing the same DVD on a regular basis, however, became monotonous. It didn't turn me off entirely, but it certainly didn't inspire me to become a regular yogi either.

When I moved to Ann Arbor in 2009, and Mark finally got me

into my regular gym routine, I was quickly introduced to hot vinyasa. My first class was a complete struggle to get through. I was not accustomed to moving and breathing in a room kept at 100 degrees, attempting to hold balancing poses that I was just learning. When my friend, who recommended that I try it, texted me to see how it went, I remember texting her back that it was the longest hour of my life! Something about that heat though... I was intrigued, and I quickly became hooked. Challenging myself to just stay for the whole class morphed into challenging myself to flow and hold balancing poses for the entire class.

Fast forward to now, over 10 years after my first hot vinyasa class, and I have now taught a few casual yoga classes to groups of friends as well as to groups of kids.

Most things in life I have learned from yoga. Patience is key. So is learning to sit with things. When I want to run, I need to stay. Holding poses for minutes at a time can be challenging, just as working through my feelings is challenging. If I focus and just *breathe* through the sensations and the feelings, I can make it to the other side. If I try to run from the sensations and feelings or take shortcuts, they will only keep coming back. **The only way out is through.**

Yoga taught me to breathe and be present. It taught me to listen to my body. It helped prevent running injuries through stretching my muscles. Most of all, it taught me that it's not about the work*out*, but the work *inward*. It's about appreciating my body for what it's able to do in that moment and trying not to think about the million things on my to-do list (something I am still working on).

So many friends say to me that they need more yoga in their life but that they just can't get their minds to slow down, or they get bored. I challenge these people, and any of you reading this, to push through that discomfort. Try a yoga class. If you don't like a certain style of yoga, try a different style. Hot vinyasa is my personal favorite, but there are so many. The benefits are numerous and so worth it.

15

Moms Demand Action & The Survivor Network

"One thing I know for sure is that bravery is contagious, and when even one lone woman stands up, it inspires so many others to do the same." – Reshma Saujani, *Brave, Not Perfect*

Where do I even begin? When Mark encouraged me to join this incredible group of people (not just women/mothers!), he never would have guessed that I would still be a part of it over 8 years later. What began as an anxious woman ranting about our gun violence crisis on Facebook, became a part-time unpaid job. One of my biggest passions in life has become saving lives by changing hearts and minds, and eventually, when our politicians develop the balls, changing laws as well.

When I joined Moms Demand Action, I held preconceived notions about the amount of work I should devote to the cause. After all, I wasn't getting paid! My views shifted, however, after attending that first conference I wrote about in the Survivor Life section. I was surrounded by like-minded people who were all dedicated to ending gun violence, some of them showing up to their state houses every single day to impress upon their legislators the severity of their choices. Suddenly the few hours a month I was devoting to my volunteer work seemed meager. I wanted to do more.

I can now say that I have held various positions within Moms Demand Action and Everytown for Gun Safety. This has taught me the importance of teaming up and supporting one another, recognizing that everyone brings something new and different to the table. It has created a strong sense of self as I understand the role that I play within my organization and my community. As the former State Chapter Lead (basically the manager of my state, helping all of the other leaders across the state of Michigan), I made sure that everyone's voices were heard. No one is more important than the other. I continue this inclusivity in my current role as a National Trainer and Mentor.

While my relationship with my fellow volunteers is strong, there is something to be said for the love and strength of our close-knit survivor community within Moms Demand Action and Everytown for Gun Safety. We always say that it is a club that no one wants to be a part of, but once you are in, you are family. I have found this to be true, and I derive comfort from every single community call or conference we have together. Granted, it is hard, as the topics are heavy, but nowhere else do I feel as understood and accepted as I do than in the survivor community; we have all been through the trauma of gun violence, in some way, shape, or form. This is not to say that my dad's suicide defines who I am, but it will always be a big part of me. Even though I am no longer a Survivor Fellow, I will always be a survivor.

16

Recovery Dharma & Meditation

"We can spend our whole lives escaping from the monsters of our minds.'" – Pema Chödrön, *When Things Fall Apart: Heart Advice for Difficult Times*

Another group I have found invaluable to my healing process is Recovery Dharma. The day that I realized I had to stop drinking because it was ruining my life – that was the day that I texted my husband and said that I was going to Alcoholics Anonymous. What I didn't know, however, is that AA is based upon religion and that there are a very specific 12 steps that must be done in a particular order. This did not jive with my spiritual beliefs and the fact that I am a notorious rule breaker.

Fortunately at my third AA meeting, which happened to be for atheists and agnostics (I'm still not sure how that works within the organization), I met a man who told me about Recovery Dharma. Recovery Dharma is for all recovering addicts, from alcohol to drugs to sex to gambling to other addictions. It is based on Buddhist principles and there is a non-linear path to recovery, very unlike the structured path of AA and their

12-step program.

My first meeting put me at ease, and I knew I was at home with this organization. The people I met reminded me of my friends in high school and college, and the diversity among the attendees was far greater than what I encountered in the few AA meetings I had attended, which were mainly gender-normative older white men and women.

The meetings also always begin with guided meditation which takes me back to my early days of meditation in Aruba, while also making me think about my reason for being there. I had begun doing daily meditation during the aforementioned Aruba vacation, and I found it to be grounding and helpful. Meditation is all mental – getting past those barriers and roadblocks in your mind that tell you that you can't focus or that make your mind race all over the place (we call it "monkey brain"). By meditating, even if you are unable to focus much, you at least give yourself time to slow your mind down while keeping your eyes closed. By the time you open your eyes, you find yourself entering a new world with an awakened sense of calm.

When I wrote this portion of my story, I had been attending Recovery Dharma meetings for four months. Almost every time at an in-person meeting, I was the first to speak during our sharing time – this is partly because I want to rid the room of the awkward silence that always ensues when the floor opens up to speak, and partly because I just want to get the words off my mind, kind of like word vomit. I have long said that I have diarrhea of the mouth (AKA no filter), and these meetings give me the perfect opportunity to share these random thoughts with non-judgmental strangers who have become my friends. We are all in the process together, fighting the good fight.

This is not to say that I don't think Alcoholics Anonymous works for many people, including friends who are also in Recovery Dharma. While I disagree with the AA statement that I do not have power over my addiction, many people live by this statement and have found that giving everything up to God is exactly the kind of faith that they need. I choose to believe that my alcohol-free lifestyle is mine and my choice only, and it is for myself that I choose to live this way. My husband, kids, friends, and family all benefit, but ultimately I realized at my very first meeting (after meeting a woman who was sober for 19 years while her kids were growing up, and then became an alcoholic again because she didn't do it for herself but for her children) that my main priority in my recovery process has to be me.

Recovery Dharma taught me that in order to have compassion and forgiveness for others, we need to recognize that their actions come from a place of pain and hurt. I have spent many sleepless nights feeling resentment toward ex-lovers and former friends, and it only hurt me. There is freedom in letting shit go and realizing that these people have their own battles and their own demons. Me holding onto the pain, hurt, and resentment only prevents *me* from moving forward. It doesn't make their lives any better or worse. It doesn't prove anything. It doesn't make us "right." It just makes us hurt more. I still haven't completely mastered this, as I still have negative feelings about certain people, but I try to let myself feel those emotions, question where/why they are coming from, and then move on. It's certainly not easy, but no one ever said life was going to be easy. Right?

17

Review

"There is no 'why me' anymore. There is just me. This is part of my healing." – Selma Blair, *Mean Baby*

What is my reason for opening up and telling you my life story and all of the trauma and drama I have experienced? By being honest and open, I am working to change the narrative around mental health. I also want to encourage frank conversation about sexual assault, through addressing my insecurities and fears head on. Bravery is defined as being scared but doing it anyway. This hasn't been a cake walk for me. However, I know that I have a gift. I have the gift of being vulnerable, even though I may be scared of what others will think of me.

My goal in my business, Bold Brave Goddess, and in telling my story, is to inspire others to be bold and brave – to go forward and tell their stories too, to be themselves unapologetically. Many friends have said to me that they don't know how I do it because they wouldn't be able to do so. I challenge **you**, especially if you are one of those friends who have made such a comment to me, to step out of your comfort zone.

Go do something crazy! Go dance in the rain, go to a party solo and strike up a conversation with a stranger, go share something personal or be vulnerable with a friend so that you can strengthen your relationship with them. You never know what could happen from getting out of your soft cushy bubble.

Now, I am not asking you to go do something STUPID, which is an entirely different story. As you've read from my past, I've done my fair share of that, too, and I wouldn't recommend it. It often happens subconsciously or by accident anyway, as I have demonstrated. What I AM doing is merely asking you to have an open mind, to just let go, and let fate take you where you are supposed to go. I have made many friendships with people who began as complete strangers, but because of my willingness to open myself up, my circle of friends is large and strong. I know that I can turn to any one of these people if I am in trouble, and for that I am sincerely grateful.

It's time for me to share everything that I have learned in my short 40+ years of life with you. Another reason for sharing my story with you is so that you can understand exactly where I am coming from and know that I did not come upon my realizations and life lessons lightly. They came to me through a lot of therapy, digging, and hard work.

My hope is that you can take away some key points from my learnings, that you can relate to them, and that you can carry this book around with you if you need some encouragement, just as I do with the book *Brave Enough* by Cheryl Strayed. Here we go!

III

Life Lessons

"The moral arc of the universe is long – too fucking long – and it bends only when forced by the strength of our raging souls." – Amanda Doyle, We Can Do Hard Things Podcast

18

Life Lesson #1: Don't put up with other people's bullshit.

"Kind and fierce can coexist." – Brené Brown, *Unlocking Us* Podcast

I made this Life Lesson #1 for a reason.

If I had a dollar for the amount of bullshit that I have dealt with over my lifetime, I would be one rich lady!

The friends I've cut out, the ex-lovers I stayed with too long, and the family members who have manipulated me have all reinforced this life lesson.

If you are in a relationship, be it friend, family, or significant other, ask yourself if you are a better person for being in it. If the answer is no, **cut that shit out of your life**. No one needs toxicity dragging them down. Unless it's your mom (or in my case, my dad before he died). Then, just create healthy boundaries. Brené Brown's popular saying reminds us that, "Daring to set boundaries is about having the courage to love ourselves, even when we risk disappointing others."

For me, setting boundaries can be especially hard because

I am a people pleaser, causing me to feel obligated to do the exact opposite of what this life lesson teaches. I like to say that I don't give a shit what anyone else thinks, when in reality, I care way too much. (Just ask my husband, who has held me many times on the sofa while I sobbed about something that I said that was misconstrued or for some blunder that I made.)

This lesson also applies to people with whom we don't have a relationship. I used to be the kind of person who would just go along with what strangers said to me, too abashed to speak up even if I questioned what someone was saying. No more of this, friends! Soon before I began writing this book, I encountered a man at the airport. I asked him no less than 3 times where something was, and he kept pointing and saying in a condescending, exasperated tone, "right over there!" like I was supposed to read his mind. Finally, I looked him in the eye and said, "Sir, I don't know where 'right over there' is." At this point, he finally became more descriptive so that I could get to where I needed to go. Sometimes you have to be forceful and pushy with people, or you will get walked on and lost (sometimes literally).

Sub-Lesson A: You can still like someone and dislike certain things that they do.

"People who are placed on pedestals are expected to pose, perfectly. Then they get knocked off when they fuck it up. I regularly fuck it up. Consider me already knocked off." – Roxane Gay, *Bad Feminist*

As I discuss later, we have a large tendency as a society to put people on pedestals, which leaves so much room for disappointment. Michael Jackson was an icon in the music industry, but the atrocities he (allegedly) committed to young boys staying at his Neverland Ranch cannot be overlooked. Despite the incriminating evidence, his fans continue to love his music, even if they are appalled by his actions. This demonstrates why it's important for us to establish boundaries around people. We don't need to keep our guard up 24/7, but we also need to remain vigilant so that others don't crush us when they unexpectedly make a bad decision or say the wrong thing.

Another recent example of this is the controversy surrounding J.K. Rowling's comments about the transgender community, and more specifically about transgender women. Rowling made a series of Tweets that sent the transgender community and its supporters up in arms. Many of her former followers lashed out at her and burned her books. Rowling followed up with her own essay attempting to explain herself, which seemed only to make matters worse. The actors portraying Rowling's main characters in the *Harry Potter* and *Fantastic Beasts* films took to social media to express their disagreement with Rowling's opinions, despite their attachments to the extensive work they did together.

This brings me to politics. In addition to public figures, so many of us have folks near and dear to our hearts with differing political opinions. They could be family members or friends believing "alternative facts," making us want to pull our hair out. Personally, I've been unfriended on social media and ostracized from family members I grew up with because of my involvement with Moms Demand Action, not to mention my bleeding-heart liberal persona. My husband and

I choose to take the high road by continuing to send holiday cards, knowing they will not be reciprocated. We still love these family members despite strongly disliking their political stance. Everyone reacts to these situations differently, and I am not here to tell you what to do, but I do ask that you remember our shared humanity.

That said, it is very likely that we will have our hearts broken more than once in our lifetime – not just by lovers but by friends and family members that we never expected. Know that it's OK to feel let down, but it's NOT OK to continue to allow said person to hurt you. That's detrimental to everyone involved.

Sub-Lesson B: Never let anyone make you feel inferior.

"In a culture where everyone is valued equally, your version is not more valuable than mine." – Rebecca Solnit, to Emma Watson on *Our Shared Shelf* interview

We are all human. Not one of us is necessarily "better" than anyone else. Society is so obsessed with titles and private societies, but what good do they do? They give those "elite" people who have large titles or bigger life accomplishments, like CEOs or sports figures, bigger egos. This results in the rest of us, those of us who don't have these titles or elite memberships, to feel "lesser than." We see these public figures as untouchables. We revere them.

Now, please don't get me wrong here. I am not saying that these titles and accomplishments and successes shouldn't be celebrated. What I *am* saying is that your status doesn't mean you get to be an asshole. Condescension doesn't look good on anyone.

I have met a handful of celebrities in my life:

Robert DeNiro & Greg Kinnear – Actors who both stayed at one of the hotels I worked for.

Bill Clinton & George W. Bush – Presidents who visited my hometown at different times.

Des Linden – Famous badass Boston marathon winner and self-proclaimed coffee connoisseur; I secretly want to be her best friend.

Shannon Watts – Kickass mom and public safety advocate who founded Moms Demand Action.

Julianne Moore – Famous actress who is actively involved with Moms Demand Action and whose daughter is on the national board of Students Demand Action.

Lucy McBath – Fierce mama whose son Jordan Davis was murdered in Florida by a racist white man, using their "Stand Your Ground" law to defend himself. Lucy went on to write a book, *Standing Our Ground*, about her son's murder. She was elected to Congress and, as of now, represents Georgia's 7th Congressional district.

Chris Murphy – Famous Connecticut Senator who held a filibuster on the Senate floor until his colleagues agreed to discuss the growing gun violence crisis. He also wrote an incredible book, *The Violence Inside Us*.

I could go on, but these are the highlights. I did not provide this list to brag, but for two reasons – to showcase these amazing human beings (other than the Presidents, as I have mixed feelings about both of them), and to tell you about my experience in meeting all of them. When I met the first half of these famous people, I was stuck in my old frame of mind that just because these people are famous and have earned accolades, they were better than me. Therefore, my body froze, my words came out shaky and I momentarily blacked out. However, when I met the second half of these celebrities, especially the politicians and activists, I knew that *I am just as good as they are*. Just because they have these titles and these glorified jobs doesn't mean that they get to treat me differently than they would their colleagues. Should they be confident in their demeanor? Absolutely. **There is a difference between being confident and being egotistical.**

19

Life Lesson #2: Don't judge other people if it doesn't directly affect you.

"It's so important for people to remember: you have no idea what's going on for someone behind closed doors. You have no idea - even the people who smile the biggest smiles and shine the brightest lights...." – Meghan Markle, *Oprah with Meghan and Harry: A CBS Primetime Special*

I almost want to repeat this one. It is so common in our society to look at other people, question them, compare ourselves, and gossip about our opinions. Unfortunately, the media promotes this. Just look at all of the celebrity gossip magazines and the entertainment/reality shows that are based on opinions, gossip, and a whole bunch of nonsense.

Hell, even Salt 'N Pepa had a song about this in the 90s. For those of you smiling and nodding right now, mad respect. For those of you too young to know what the fuck I'm talking about, it's a song called, "None of Your Business." What you do is no one else's damn business and vice versa. (Now I'm going to have that song stuck in my head for the rest of the night, but I digress....)

While I know this is hard to do, I challenge you to ignore or even question those who judge or gossip out loud. I once heard of someone who wore a rubber band around her wrist, and when she caught herself saying something negative about someone else, she snapped the rubber band to feel the pain. It's so easy to get talking and let the conversation slide into negativity and gossip. The fact is, the people who we are talking about are not there to defend themselves, and we have no way of truly knowing their side of the story.

Now I am most certainly not perfect when it comes to this, and I am not claiming to be a saint. I have talked about people behind their backs, but I am not proud of that fact. What I have learned over the years when talking about someone else is to share the information that I know. Instead of saying, "Ugh, this person is running so late. How inconsiderate and irresponsible," I can say, "I am irritated that this person is running late." Then I can find something to keep myself busy until the person shows up and find out WHY they were running late. (Also, I am notoriously late, so I apologize if you are reading this and it is resonating....)

The exception is of course when we truly are affected by someone's choices or actions. While I hesitate to mention it, because it has become so politicized when it boils down to public safety, the recent aversion to wearing masks and vaccinating ourselves to protect those around us is the first thing that comes to mind here. Medical exemptions aside, it absolutely pisses me off when people selfishly decide not to vaccinate themselves until they end up sick. Many of the lives lost during the COVID pandemic could have been saved by a simple poke of a needle, with minor side effects considering the alternative. Before my kids could get vaccinated, I was scared shitless of having to take them to the doctor, or God forbid, the emergency room because they were all filled to the brim with uber sick people capable of infecting my kids. So yes, thank you very much, I will judge you for making poor life choices that affect me and especially my precious children.

Sub-Lesson A: If someone else's actions bother you, ask yourself why.

"I don't have to explain myself to you
   I am a grown woman and I do what I want to do." – Adele, in "Oh My God," by Adele Adkins and Greg Kurstin

Something that has helped me, that I have heard from many social media influencers, is to question *why* I feel strongly about something that someone does or posts. If my initial reaction is negative, I ask myself why and where it might be coming from. It forces me to slow down and rethink before saying anything I might regret. And trust me, I am the queen of impulsivity. Yoga and meditation have helped keep some knee-jerk reactions at bay, but it's still a struggle at times.

   For a long time, I was impatient and embarrassed with the way that my mother-in-law orders her food in a restaurant. Her meat and her eggs have to be well done, and she always reminds the waitstaff of this after she's already ordered. Internally, I would roll my eyes and secretly hope that her food would be undercooked just to spite her idiosyncrasy. Several years later and through much self reflection, I found myself questioning why in the world I would think this way, as I wouldn't want anyone to wish malice upon *me*. I think the answer lies in my former impatience and narrow-minded temperament, which I have vastly improved upon only through years of therapy and meditation. (For the record, I love my mother-in-law, and we have a great relationship....Yeah, I could see where some of you with monsters-in-law may have been going with this, but fortunately I don't have one of those beasts!)

Outside of our immediate circles, we are exposed to the inner lives of everyone and their mothers on social media. Many celebrities bare their souls on there. While some of the comments they receive are kind and empathic, some are just downright awful. As my dear friend Trisha likes to say, "It costs $0 to keep scrolling." If a celebrity posing nude or making a statement makes you feel a certain type of way, stop for a second. *Breathe.* Why does it annoy you so much? Why do you want to comment? Will your comment accomplish anything? If so, by all means, go ahead. If you are standing up for something that you believe strongly in, great. But if your response is hurtful or mean-spirited, maybe sit on it for a day and see if you still want to respond that way.

This lesson has taught me so much about myself. I have begun questioning many of the automatic thoughts that flood my brain when I encounter a new idea/person/situation. If I can pinpoint *why* my brain thinks the way that it does, I can begin to change it. By doing this, I have also cultivated friendships. When I ignore my brain's initial judgements (NOT intuition – that's something entirely different, covered in Life Lesson #4) about a person next to me, I can initiate a conversation. While I know that it's not true, my brain frequently tells me that the fierce woman next to me is prettier/better/more talented than me, and I am therefore intimidated to introduce myself.

However, true to my commitment to be brave, I inevitably strike up a conversation. More often than not, I discover another bold brave goddess, and if I am lucky, they become my friend. If I hadn't asked myself why I was feeling a certain way and let myself be intimidated, I would have a lot fewer friends, and that would be my great loss.

Sub-Lesson B: Don't let other people's choices get under your skin and don't try to correct them.

"All my life, people have either questioned what I am or they've tried to tell me what I am. This is my thing: Who am I to tell somebody what they are? And likewise, who are you to tell me who I am? What you believe about yourself, you are." – Mei Campanella, in "African" from *One Drop: Shifting the Lens on Race*, by Dr. Yaba Blay

I see this shit in yoga or workout classes all the time. Someone is minding their own business doing their own thing, when the instructor notices them and calls them out. Instead of asking why said person is modifying their exercise (as long as they are not using improper form which could result in injury) or resting their body, the instructor assumes the worst or is offended that this person is not doing exactly what they said. But without asking the person, how the hell could the instructor know what is going on with this person's body? They could have an injury or they could just not be feeling it that day. Whatever it is, it really doesn't fucking matter to anyone but that person.

People also tend to get themselves all worked up over others' wardrobe choices. When it comes to attire, what does it matter what someone else puts on their body? When I notice myself beginning to get judgey (if that's not a word, I just made it up) about someone's clothing (or lack thereof), I stop and remind myself to just look away. Don't like someone's thong? Look away sister. Feel offended by someone's t-shirt? Well, it's a free country, and people do offensive shit all the time. Take the high road and look away. We can be especially compassionate when we notice a youngster wearing the most weather inappropriate clothing, because chances are, that little heathen dressed themselves and the caregiver was not about to fight that battle.

So often, we find ourselves getting involved or personally offended by other people's life choices when it really shouldn't matter to us. I learned in 2017 that I have several food intolerances, the main one being gluten. How many freaking times have I had to explain to people over the past several years that, no, I can't eat that cookie or try that bread because the results will leave me hunched over in pain?! Some people choose to take this personally as if my digestive system is choosing to discriminate specifically against their homemade banana bread. By changing my diet around, I have made my former constant suffering disappear, only to add the stress of having to explain my food intolerances to people. My favorite *insert eye roll here* is when I list off my food intolerances, and folks respond by saying, "What DO you eat?," to which I invariably respond, "Everything else." Good grief. As if my eating choices affect their everyday life.

Let's look at an example of yours truly discovering the importance of this lesson the hard way. There was an embarrassing race incident I once had where I noticed the bib number on the girl next me, and I told her that it wasn't her turn yet. She quickly corrected me to say that she was a survivor of whatever cause it was (frankly I forget now, as this was several years ago), and she was going to be kicking off the race. Instead of saying, "I'm so sorry," my dumb ass kept talking and digging myself further into a hole. It taught me to keep my damn mouth shut and not make stupid assumptions about people. Here I thought I was putting this girl "in her place," when in reality she had to put me in mine. Sheesh. The world would be much better off if people weren't constantly nit-picking at each other and trying to "correct" each other. Perhaps the next time you find yourself getting irritated with the way someone is living their life, if you MUST say something, make it something kind and empathic. You may find out the reason why, and you will come out wiser on the other side.

Sub-Lesson C: Learn to live with other people's idiosyncrasies and don't let your irritation get the best of you.

"Some people work at being miserable. I work at being happy."
– Dolly Parton, to Oprah.com

I know, I know. I hear you. This is much easier said than done, as are a lot of my pieces of advice. But wouldn't you be such a happier and more chill person if you could just accept people for who they are? I spent way too many years of my marriage letting my husband's idiosyncrasies get under my skin (the number of socks I've had to pick up from the floor over the past 15 years must be in the millions by now). I would feel angry or annoyed and sometimes even blow up at him, even though they are just part of who he is. With marriage therapy and a lot of spiritual healing on my part, I have learned to just accept him and know that he is doing the same for me.

After all, I guarantee you that you annoy other people too! No one person acts the exact same as someone else (except for those twins in that crazy reality TV show that I saw a clip of, but that's just fucking creepy). Again, it is so natural for us to react negatively to things that are not in our comfort zone. We think other people are "weird" when they are just *different* than us. They were raised in a completely different way by completely different parents and perhaps in a completely different culture.

We seriously need to check our cultural views at the door. Many of us are so quick to judge the way that people from other cultures (and even just differing backgrounds) act, when we have no idea how they were raised. Instead of letting their different mannerisms and traditions bother us, we can just let them be as they are. Better yet, we could learn about them! For many people in this country, English is their second language, and the transition to a new culture is already hard enough. Too often, complete strangers feel the need to offer unsolicited opinions or just show a complete lack of empathy to the struggles of others. I better not ever fucking hear someone say that our nation's immigrants should just return to their own country! Someone once said this to a local business owner and friend, and this interaction made the national news. The local business owner was merely speaking to a school group about the racism that he and his children have encountered in the US after moving here from Mexico many years ago. Some white asshole thought he would "put him in his place" and tell him to go back to Mexico. Let me tell you, the response was inspiring. Not only did said asshole get disowned by his own son, but the business owner and his fabulous restaurant called *Chela's*, received an increase in business and numerous cards of support.

While this is not where I was necessarily planning on going with this, and I jumped on my political soapbox for a minute, it just demonstrates how someone's irritation with other cultures can impact not only a whole community but the entire world. My husband's employee down in Mexico even heard the story of our business owner friend on the news and called to tell Mark to give him his best.

I am glad that brave activists are bringing these issues to light and creating platforms for those who are disenfranchised, but at the same time, I am sad that people are still growing up in our country and letting race and culture influence what they think of others. After all, if we don't look deep inside of ourselves and delve into why traits about certain people bother us so much, these thoughts can truly spin out of control and destroy an entire society.

Sub-Lesson D: Everything is not as it seems.

"The concept of privilege makes the world seem less safe. We want to protect our vision of a world that is fair and kind and predictable." – Ijeoma Oluo, *So you want to talk about race*

Oftentimes we develop preconceived notions about what others are experiencing in their lives. Especially in the age of social media, we see what others are posting online – seeing only beautiful pictures and stories – when in reality, we don't know what is going on behind the scenes. This is exactly why we should not judge others or make assumptions. For all we know, for all of those perfect Instagram or Pinterest photos, there is something going on behind the scenes of which we are completely unaware. Be careful what you say, and never assume to know what is going on in someone else's life.

Likewise, some people find it easy to fake confidence, hence the saying, "Fake it till you make it!" Just because someone *sounds* like they know what they're doing doesn't actually mean that they know what the fuck they are doing. My husband is a perfect example of this. It took me a while to catch on, and he still fools me occasionally, but he tends to make up a reasonable-sounding answer on the spot if you ask him a question and he has no idea. This begs the question – if he can do it, why can't I? Better yet, if most men can do this, why can't we women? We tend to second guess ourselves so much more so than our male-identified counterparts. For more on this, see Life Lesson 4B.

20

Life Lesson #3: Be flexible, and don't let setbacks discourage you.

"I didn't even think for a second that I would fail; I just really thought to myself, 'I have to do this.'" – Kate Roberts, "Kate Roberts: The Women's Health Maverick," *The Dissenters* Podcast

We all know this one. We've all heard it before. The reason I am writing it this very moment is because I was just about to sit down and type, after taking a month off for the holidays, when my husband called me to tell me that our eldest son wore his boots to tennis instead of his tennis shoes. After rolling my eyes and being momentarily irritated, I sucked it up and offered to bring his tennis shoes to him. I am fortunate that I have this ability – this *flexibility* – in my job to do these kinds of things. In fact, I forget to pack things in bookbags all the time and am forced to re-work my schedule around dropping things off at schools. Such is mom life – and I love and cherish every minute of it!

Being flexible can apply to so many things in life. It certainly

applies to my workouts, especially my running and yoga practice. I have sustained several injuries and still have an ongoing
shoulder injury, thanks to carrying around my youngest son
when he was a roly-poly baby. The first running injury that I
incurred was in my left hip, after getting a personal record in
a 5K because I was determined to beat my husband (although
now he smokes me, and I don't even stand a chance keeping
up with him). At the time, I was somewhat new to running
and working out, and I was convinced I would instantly lose
my muscle tone and gain weight if I didn't keep working out
practically every day, despite any pain or injuries I had. So
what did I do? I kept going to the gym, putting pressure and
pain on my hip. Instead of resting or being open-minded to
different exercises that wouldn't strain my injury, I stubbornly
continued my regular workout routine. This exacerbated my
injury and landed me in physical therapy. My hip bothered me
for years afterward. Had I been kinder to myself and rested, I
likely could have healed and avoided the physical therapy.

Most companies and entrepreneurs know all about being
flexible and having to make changes in order to be successful.
As of my writing this paragraph, I am only 3 months into my
business, and I have already had to reassess my goals and some
of my visions. That is OK. As we learn, we grow. **As we learn, we
change.** If we are so stuck in our initial ideas, we would never
move forward.

A huge learning curve for me has been understanding that
I have to be kind to myself when I realize that I can't always
accomplish everything I said I would. If this happens to you,
apologize and take ownership of letting that commitment go.
There have been many times where I over-commit myself
or book my schedule to the max, only to realize that I am

double-booked, or I just can't handle one more meeting. It is then that I must swallow my pride and send that message or make that phone call to cancel a commitment. We can't be so determined to do everything we said we would, that when we are feeling overwhelmed, we just keep plugging along despite our exhaustion. This will just cause burn out, for which you can reference Life Lesson #9.

There is a yoga mantra that says, "Let go of expectations." When you are open to new possibilities and new ways of doing things, you are not going to get stuck in your head as we often do. If we get too stuck on one path, thinking that path and only that path can lead us to our desired destination, we are not only going to be sorely disappointed, but we may never even reach our destination. There are so many "right" ways of doing things. **Don't get too stuck in your own head!**

Sub-Lesson A: Focus on the solutions, not the problem.

"I want to be free more than I want to be mad." – Alicia Garza, quoted in a *The Cut* article later used in Rebecca Traister's *Good and Mad: The Revolutionary Power of Women's Anger*

This is something I have had to repeat over and over to myself during COVID. It's become one of my mantras. When my mind is spinning because the problem is so great, I take a deep breath (I always take a deep breath first, to which my friend Ashley can attest) and remind myself of the end goal. Since I have so many passions, it is so easy for me to get swept up in the negativity and the weight of the world on my shoulders. I must then remind myself that I am working hard to be the light and "the change [I] wish to see," as the wise Ghandi once said. Set your sight on the prize and make baby steps to get there. Any progress is progress! As Marie Forleo promises in her book of the same title, "Everything is figureoutable!"

When I joined Moms Demand Action, I was asked to take on the leadership role of entering information into our database. I can freely admit that I was horrible at this job, as data and numbers are NOT my passion (I like to blame my dyscalculia). However, I was smart enough to know that if I trained someone else in this position who WAS good at it, I could transition to something that I could excel in. A position opened up to help plan events for the organization, which I knew I would enjoy based on my previous hotel sales and events experience. I nominated one of the people I had "trained" (I say this loosely, since he did a lot of his own research) to do the data entry so that I could volunteer for this events role, which was accepted with open arms. I am proud to say that person went on to handle data entry for our entire state because he is *so* good at what he does. Instead of dwelling on the fact that I sucked at data entry, I used my delegating skills so that I could focus on what I AM good at. As Mark likes to say, "Problem presented, problem solved."

Sub-Lesson B: Things come and go as they need to.

"You will never be understood by everyone. Most people are still trying to understand themselves. The things you want to achieve are yours, and the people who try to push you into a corner aren't worth having in your life." – Courtney Peppernell, *I Hope You Stay*

Things are brought into your life as they need to be. A few years ago, I participated in a Zoom meeting with 3 amazing sober people like myself, and it made me realize just how much I needed the support at that very moment. I needed to hear the words that were said, and I needed to express my own energy and pour my heart out. When I typed this after the Zoom meeting, I still had tears gleaming in my eyes.

Each of us spoke on the call about what we were working on, and I realized that the thing I need to work on the most is doing things for myself and actually sitting still. When I explained how much I am doing for others and my constant to-do list, the leader of the group asked me what I am running from. My initial answer was, "I don't know; I feel like I am attacking everything head-on." After much back and forth, I admitted to running from something. It dawned on me that I don't sit well because sitting still for me means not being in control. Frequently during Zoom meetings, I long to get up and walk around or be the one doing the talking, but instead I am forced to sit. (Then it's like I am back on the volleyball bus again with my molester and I can't get up because he is next to me with his hand up my shorts – a true example of PTSD showing up in unexpected ways.)

This sober Zoom call led me to the realization that my therapist was not providing me with the support that I needed, nor was she treating me with the respect I deserve because she was constantly distracted with her phone. This was not fair to me, hence why I think that this sobriety group came along at just the right moment for me so that I could recognize my need for a more supportive therapist. The people involved were committed to learning about themselves and bettering themselves. While I soon-after left the group (after discovering that it was yet another multi-level marketing scheme), it was exactly what I needed in that moment. Then when I was ready, I let it go.

21

Life Lesson #4: Always listen to your gut.

"We have all the answers buried inside us, and our issue isn't that we *just don't know*, it's that we *just don't know we know*."
– Holly Whitaker, *Quit Like a Woman: The Radical Choice to Not Drink in a Culture Obsessed with Alcohol*

Whenever I think of this life lesson, a story comes back to haunt me. I read a story about a woman once who escaped death in a parking garage. She went to use the bathroom by herself and *didn't listen to her gut* when it told her that there was a sketchy man nearby. She barely made it out alive and shared her story to showcase how important that little voice in our head is, and we mustn't ignore it.

Another example is Cheryl Strayed, where she discusses her gut reactions to a particular man she encountered on her Pacific Coast Trail hike in her book *Wild* – how he struck her as creepy but then her mind told her that she was just being silly, until he indeed intruded on her privacy and showed his true colors. Cheryl and the woman described above were lucky in their escape from horrific things happening to them. Many others who ignore their intuition are not here to tell their stories.

Because the first woman's story will forever be ingrained in my brain, I have always trusted my gut. One late night when I pulled up to my bank's ATM and there was a man approaching my car, something didn't feel right about the situation. I decided to drive off and not take any chances; I could pull out cash the next day. We must trust ourselves when that gnawing feeling is there, warning us that the person near us doesn't have the best of intentions. It's so important that we listen to it. Instead of telling ourselves we are "just being silly," we should absolutely run away as fast as we can and not look back. It is much better to be silly than hurt or dead. And for the record, it's NOT silly. We have gut reactions for this very reason, friends. It's only in today's society that we have begun to question them. Our ancient ancestors (think the time of wooly mammoths and saber-toothed tigers) certainly didn't, as they knew that their lives depended on their guts and their intuitions, and those who didn't run from danger didn't make it to the next day.

With social media making it so easy to stalk people, we have to be even more careful. One day I received a direct message from a man whose profile read "humble and trusted." My initial subconscious thought was that he must be a creeper, but the part of my brain trying to rationalize things told me to just be nice and respond. However, when the man started getting snarky with me for not responding in two seconds and had the audacity to ask if I speak English, I blocked that mofo! It became clear to me that his intentions were not copacetic.

When Ann Curry became co-anchor of the *Today* show in 2011, I was one of her biggest cheerleaders. Seeing a minority woman in a position of power made my heart happy. However, as you may remember, she abruptly left this role just over one year later in 2012. Something about her departure *didn't feel right*. The way that Matt Lauer handled things and just his entire demeanor didn't sit well with me. Therefore, it was no surprise to me when it was revealed in 2017 that he was a serial harasser/assaulter. My gut reactions were affirmed, and I found myself thinking that karma found its way to this asshole. For my Life Lesson on karma, see Life Lesson #10. (And if you want to see how a true bold brave goddess handles such situations, look up Ann Curry's reaction to Matt Lauer's firing.)

My husband will also tell you that my mama gut is always right. I can tell the difference between strep throat, a cold, and an unexplained fever due to a virus before even taking my children to the doctor. Somehow this doesn't work on myself however, as my brain likes to tell me I'm dying when, in reality, I just have a weird benign rash (pityriasis) or yeast in my eye (look it up; it's a thing).

Mark has also always said, "If something is too good to be true, it likely is." So when a company approached me on Instagram and told me that they would post my picture for a nominal fee so that I could get 1000 followers within a week, even though **my gut** told me that I should first check in with my husband for his opinion, I ignored that intuition and signed up. I thought, "what's the worst that could happen?" Well, I'll tell you what – it wasted a lot of my time, because I learned that all of these so-called followers I was getting were not actually people but just bots created by people overseas. Having a bunch of fake followers on my Instagram account doesn't vibe with me. I learned that I would have to work for each follower, by posting, using hashtags, and just being my true authentic unapologetic self.

All of this said, if you aren't doing what's right, your body will tell you. When you know you are defying your gut, you feel icky, you feel unsettled, you feel *not right.* Your body is literally screaming at you to back the eff up and do what it was originally telling you to do. **Listen to it.**

Sub-Lesson A: Your subconscious is stronger than you think.

"Be careful what you wish for. Sometimes the universe listens like a child does to her parent." – Nikita Gill, "Wildest Wish" Poem

Once I became sober and attended weekly therapy and Dharma Recovery sessions for several months, I thought I had worked through most of the issues in my past. Little did I know that I was subconsciously holding onto some ridiculous idea that I was alone standing in a kitchen at the age of 5 making myself breakfast. This is what I uncovered through a video reiki session with my dear friend Tia, and yes, I am being completely serious. I believe that there is an aura that each of us emanates, and clearly she picked up on this through the computer. Through all of the distance between us, she could sense that I was broken inside. She asked me to reflect back on myself as a little girl, and I just kept seeing myself standing alone in my grandparents' kitchen trying to make myself some scrambled eggs in the microwave. *At age 5.* Tia helped guide me through this feeling of loneliness as tears dripped down my face. With my eyes completely closed, Tia instructed my current self to take the hand of my 5-year-old self and tell her that it will be OK. We went off to another place and two suddenly became one, and I became whole again.

If you are not into this kind of thing, I am sure that this sounds completely hokey and made up. I know how I felt though. That's one thing that I never forget – how things make me feel. There is a reason that the quote by Maya Angelou is so famous, "People will forget what you said, people will forget what you did, but people will never forget how you made them feel." I turn to this quote time and time again as I remember things from my past. I may have inherited my mom's incredible ability to "forget" (or at least put in the very back trenches of my mind) the shitty things that people said or did to me, but there is no way in hell that my body will ever forget the feelings that they gave me. They are all stored in my subconscious, and when triggered, they surface. **This keeps me from repeating past mistakes.**

Sub-Lesson B: Question others' advice before taking it. Dig deep to discover what YOU really need.

"I am not an angry girl
    But it seems like I've got everyone fooled
    Every time I say something they find hard to hear
    They chalk it up to my anger
    And never to their own fear" – Ani DiFranco, in "Not a Pretty Girl," written by Ani DiFranco

Sometimes others have their own best interests in mind and won't consider yours. This is the harsh reality. Friends stab friends in the back to move forward in life. While I certainly agree that we should love with an open heart and give all of ourselves to people, we must do so with caution. If we just blindly and naively shared our whole hearts with the world, they would quickly get crushed. I see it happen all the time to people on social media. These brave souls bare their innermost thoughts, and some asshole comes along to make a nasty comment and stick their nose where it doesn't belong. *Sigh*. Such is the 21st century. Well, it was always this way, but now it's just more accessible to judge and gossip about others since it's online for everyone to see, and the asshole hides behind the anonymity of their screen.

Also, remember that just because you have a bunch of sup-porters to do or say something doesn't mean that you should. I've often had multiple people agree on things I should do in my relationship, but I have to remember that they are not the ones married to my husband. While I find their input valuable and they of course have the best of intentions, I have learned to reflect on their words and not blindly follow everything they say. Instead, I determine if it's something I should implement or just keep doing what I know will keep the peace at home. Sometimes it's better to sit one out or hold your tongue. I've had arguments with Mark that I know my friends would totally back me up on (cuz that's what friends do), but for the greater good of our marriage, I bite my tongue and just let Mark win the argument. But trust me (and Mark would agree), I am no pushover!!

Sub-Lesson C: Know your truth.

"Anything is possible if you're living in your truth." – Dr. Yaba Blay, *One Drop: Shifting the Lens on Race*

I always think of Vince Vaughn's character in *Couples Retreat* when I say to myself, "I know my truth," which makes me giggle. But it's real. It's valid. Only **I** know what I have been through and what's happened to me, and I won't let anyone tell me otherwise.

You, too, are the only one responsible for your own knowledge and your learned experience. I recently sat on yet another Zoom call, thanks to the pandemic, where licensed therapists had to remind the young audience that only they themselves can define what is traumatizing for them. The same goes for all aspects of our lives. A meme I saw once said, "Strange, isn't it? You know yourself better than anyone else, yet you crumble at the words of someone who hasn't even lived a second of your life. **Focus on your own voice**, it's the only one that matters." Mic drop.

22

Life Lesson #5: Tell your personal story if and when you feel comfortable doing so.

"If we live in secret shame we are eroding our own power." - Ilyse Hogue, "How to Inspire Hope with Ilyse Hogue," *Permission to Speak* Podcast

I realize that not everyone is an open book like me. Being honest and open is something that has always come naturally to me – just ask my mother. In high school, when she asked me if I used protection with my boyfriend, I replied that "all 6 condoms worked." There was also the time that I shoplifted and told on myself, henceforth telling on my friends, too (sorry friends). It's no wonder my eldest son is the same way – he is constantly turning himself in and admitting to his misdeeds. It is endearing though.

By telling your personal story, you become relatable. We have this weird tendency as humans to feel like our most intimate stories must only belong to us, and therefore, we should keep them to ourselves. We feel a sense of embarrassment if we are disgusted or appalled with ourselves about something we said or did. We somehow feel that we are unlike the rest of society, and everyone will be totally turned off if we reveal our true selves. The fact is, the experiences that we have are all things that have happened to people before us and will continue to happen to people after us. **There is beauty in sharing our mistakes**, our errors, our trauma, so that others who are going through the same thing can relate and feel a sense of community. It is up to those of us who are bold and brave enough to speak up to do so, so that we can be the voices for the millions of others who are suffering silently.

Something that my friend, Jon Gold, taught me is that statistics are not as effective in motivating people as are personal stories. We both spoke at a Moms Demand Action meeting, which occurred immediately following the Parkland, FL shooting when our membership grew by tenfold. I was new to sharing my story and public speaking. When our leader at the time asked me to retell my intimate survivor story, I told her that I didn't feel comfortable doing so, and I instead got up in front of 250 people and shared statistics from the Everytown for Gun Safety website about suicide. Jon spoke after me, where *he* shared his intimate survivor story as well as his life journey transitioning from NRA trainer to Moms Demand Action leader. His words still reverberate in my head to this day, and never again will I share mere statistics without also sharing my personal story.

Sub-Lesson A: Your story is just as important as others.

"What we do and the way we move people is not for us to define or fully know." – Chanel Miller, "Chanel Miller Promises: We are Never Stuck," *We Can Do Hard Things* Podcast

It took me some time to understand this concept. When I joined Moms Demand Action and began telling my survivor story, I didn't feel like it even compared to the stories of the grieving mothers who lost their children to gun violence. That's exactly the problem though – I was comparing myself to others, breaking my own rule (see Life Lesson #14C).

While it may be true that some stories are more tragic or more powerful than yours, it does NOT make yours less valuable. (Remember we talked about this in Life Lesson #1B? No one is inferior to anyone else!) Each time we tell our story, it impacts someone else in some way, whether we know it or not. The biggest satisfaction that I get from sharing my story is when people tell me that I inspired them to tell their own story. That is my main goal – to encourage others to be brave and unabashedly share their stories too.

Now this is where my mom says, "There are some things you just don't talk about." I say *bullshit*. If you aren't going to talk about hard things, who will? Why feel alone in your suffering when you can speak up and be surrounded by people who are going through the same thing? There is no need to feel shame. If anything, feel bold and powerful that you are strong enough to tell your truth.

I told my mom that this quote of hers is going into my book, to which she laughed. However, when I explained to her that through my candidness, I have had so many people open up to me and share things with me that they normally would not, she understood. We began talking more about my dad, and before I knew it, she was sharing more of her story with me. There is something beautiful in being vulnerable, my friends.

Arguably one of the most vulnerable, courageous women to tell her story is Chanel Miller, quoted at the beginning of this section. In that same podcast with the Doyle sisters, she also said, "I don't think we will ever, ever fully realize what we mean to other people." I think what Chanel means in her wise-beyond-her-years words is that our impact on people is so profound that we can't begin to unpack it. Chanel is a champion for sexual assault survivors by so openly telling her story to let others know they are not alone. To let others know that their stories, too, matter.

23

Life Lesson #6: Our mistakes are invaluable learning opportunities.

"Making mistakes is cool. There seems to be this misconception that making mistakes makes you weak, or stupid, or somehow less of a person, but the truth is, making mistakes brings you one step closer to success." – Lilly Singh, *How to Be a Bawse: A Guide to Conquering Life*

Mark likes to remind me of the quote "As emotion goes up, intellect goes down." After all, if there were a queen of emotion, I'd be wearing the motherfucking crown! My strong emotions have been at the heart of so many impulsive decisions, and they have resulted not only in scoldings by my family members and both of my husbands, but also in natural consequences. I am only now just beginning to slow down and trying to process things before letting my emotions make immediate decisions for me.

Over the past few years, I have really fucked up. I've made decisions that have left me crying in a heap on the floor, or my mind spinning out of control while mentally beating myself up. The thing is, every time that happened, it helped me grow. Because I never want to relive those painful moments which, of course, feel like an eternity at the time, I choose to use the knowledge and lessons bestowed upon me to improve myself.

My father-in-law called me one day to say that he and my mother-in-law were locked out of their house, so he needed me to come over and let them in since I had a spare key, and they live only 10 minutes away. Instead of quickly checking out of the grocery store and driving over there, I called my sister-in-law who lives 30 minutes away to ask her if she could go let them in instead. I had asked my father-in-law if he had called her and he said no. I selfishly thought, "Why not? She doesn't have any babies who need to nap." I worked it out with her that she would go let her parents back in their house, since I was grocery shopping and my youngest needed to nap.

When I got home, after sauntering through the store and taking my sweet time, I called my father-in-law to make sure that he and my mother-in-law were safely inside and warm. He was incredibly angry with me, rightfully so. He then revealed to me that my sister-in-law had been driving around that very morning taking care of her friend who was sick with cancer. *Shit*, did I feel guilty! I was so self-absorbed that all I could think about was my grocery shopping and my son's nap, which by the way, he decided to boycott that day anyway. So, while my son boycotted his nap, I ugly cried and questioned my life decisions.

What I learned from this experience was that I needed to be more flexible, going back to Life Lesson #3. Then when my husband called me because our son forgot his tennis shoes, the old me would have just made him come back home for them instead of offering to take them to him. The old me got so bent out of shape by these small setbacks and inconveniences while the wiser, more experienced me just lets it roll off of my shoulders knowing that this is just part of life.

Another valuable mistake happened when I first began working in hotel sales. I got too excited about making more and more phone calls and in-person visits that I neglected to follow up properly with those connections via e-mail as I promised them I would. Instead of immediately sending them the information we discussed, I put it off for weeks until I had about 20 people who were waiting on said information from me. Not one of them e-mailed me back after I had procrastinated for 2 weeks. It was a sad and glaringly obvious lesson that I had to learn early on —when focusing on these intimate connections, complete things from start to finish, or you will quickly lose your fans.

I also vividly remember my last days working with my hotel sales mentor Karen. I was young and cocky, and I thought I had found a better opportunity elsewhere (which actually turned out to be a total nightmare). Because I thought I had nothing to lose, I had no qualms about going into our general manager's office and telling him exactly what I thought of him (which, you can guess, was not a glowing review) while letting him know that I had an offer somewhere else. The next day, Karen called me, and I quietly sat in my car while she gently scolded me about burning bridges. I still like to think from the glimmer in her voice, though, that she was secretly happy that I told my asshole boss off. He intimidated a lot of people and made them feel inferior, which just made me more defiant.

In my case, I am fortunate that I didn't hurt my future in hotel sales when I gave my boss a piece of my mind, but in many cases, this does happen to people. The power of your words goes a long way, either positively or negatively. However, I do believe that if you are being your authentic self and speaking truths, you likely will be just fine. Perhaps that is why my mistake never came back to bite me. Nevertheless, I was definitely more cautious going forward.

Sub-Lesson A: Forgiving yourself is key.

"For me, becoming isn't about arriving somewhere or achieving a certain aim. I see it instead as forward motion, a means of evolving, a way to reach continuously toward a better self. The journey doesn't end." – Michelle Obama, *Becoming*

I have learned more about forgiveness in the past 5 years, in my sobriety, than I did my whole life before it. While I have struggled with the key component – to forgive myself – I have at least begun the path. I struggle every day while reflecting on poor decisions I once made...driving drunk, hiding empty wine bottles, seeing my eldest find my puke bucket next to the guest bed when I was too belligerent to sleep next to my husband...These things are so painful, but as I type them, I feel some release. They were part of me, *but they do not define me*. I can leave them behind. That is why they are in the past.

If other inspirational recovered people who have gone before me are able to forgive themselves, why can't I? Why am I any less deserving? In listening to multiple Brené Brown and Glennon Doyle podcasts, a common theme surfaces that **we are not defined by our biggest mistakes**. I want you to think about the most terrible thing you have ever done. Really dig deep, below the surface. More than likely, it is painful to recall. Where are you now, versus where you were when you made that bad decision? Chances are, you have come a long way and are no longer in that space. You don't identify with that portion of your past. So why then, do we dwell on this shit? Why do we let it eat us up and refuse to just fucking let it go? Friends, I am asking this on behalf of all of us, myself included.

It seems to me that once you are able to own up to your experiences and forgive yourself, it is that much easier for others to do the same. Besides, it is not your fault how people react to you, and you shouldn't beat yourself up and relive your experiences repeatedly. Forgive yourself and move on, sister.

24

Life Lesson #7: Personal connections are so important. Don't underestimate them, but also understand that not everyone is going to like you, and that's OK.

"Baby girl, we don't change. We take the gravel in the shell and we make a pearl. We help other people to change so that they can see more kinds of beauty." – P!nk, to her daughter, on *MTV VMAs*

It doesn't matter if you are Oprah – what you have to offer just isn't going to resonate with everyone. I try to put out all of the right energy and do all the right things, but that doesn't stop people from unfriending me on Facebook while being friendly (AKA, *fake*) to my face. There are always going to be people like this.

My absolute favorite mentor in the hotel business was my National Director of Sales, Karen, at the first major hotel I worked at out of college. Here I was promoted quite quickly from Restaurant Manager to Sales Manager, as my upper management observed that my skill set would be more useful in the sales office working with clients, versus trying to manage seasoned employees in the restaurant (at which I was terrible). Karen flew in to help train me and take me out to visit customers. We actually got kicked out of an office right away, which was a funny introduction into making in-person cold calls. Anyway, while driving to one of our client visits, Karen asked me what percentage of people I thought liked me. I told her 90%, and she laughed at my cockiness. I wish that I could remember what she told me is the average since I can't seem to find any reliable information on this online, but I CAN tell you that I still like to think that my average is higher than most. Perhaps it's my "glass half full" attitude, but even Karen admitted that perhaps my number is 80%. I believe in myself! And for those who don't, well, they can read my Life Lessons # 1 and #2.

Because I had such high opinions of myself, I spent a lot of time in my twenties, and arguably into my mid-thirties, trying to make myself likable. I will speak more to this in Life Lesson #14. For now, though, I'll just say that **expecting nearly everyone to like you will only flood you with disappointment**.

Outside of the work atmosphere, I want to stress how important it is to be self-aware and open to connections. You never know who you might be talking to – it could be someone helping you or vice versa. If you are constantly buried in your phone (hey, I'm totally guilty of this too sometimes friends), you aren't attracting any open conversations or positive energy. You might be too busy looking at pictures of your friends' dogs to find out that your Lyft driver is a business owner who might help you with YOUR business, or the woman sitting next to you on the plane is another social justice warrior just like you. Yes, these things have happened to me, but only because I was open to receiving them. My friend Maria, in fact, likes to say that certain meetings and connections would "only happen to Celeste." For a while I thought she might be right and that I'm super cool and special, but when I hear my Everytown survivor friends' stories and how they are out there meeting the same kind of influential people and doing things that others could only dream of, I realized that no, it's actually our hard work and our effort that puts us in these positions. We may attract some of these connections because of who we are, but we have also suffered a lot and worked hard to get to exactly where we are today.

Sub-Lesson A: You will have haters.

"Repeat after me:
    I will honor myself by being brave enough to be disliked. I am not for everyone, even if I'm amazing. Everyone is not for me."
– Nedra Tawwab, on her Instagram account @nedratawwab

You better believe it. And not just the strangers and social media bullies, but people who you thought were on your side. People who you thought were your friends. They may gaslight and manipulate you, all to make you start questioning yourself, your motives, and your sanity. You may even begin doubting if you are truly a good person.

STOP RIGHT THERE. Take a look in the mirror. Connect with some genuine sincere friends, people who truly know you. They will tell it to you like it is. Those who have your best interest at heart and not just their own. You will start to learn that certain people, while they made you feel good and possibly even loved and understood at the beginning of your relationship with them, are only in it for themselves. Perhaps they enjoyed being your confidante and pretending to care so deeply about you that you quickly considered them to be one of your best friends. After some time, however, they slowly started infiltrating your mind with their manipulative ways.

It is people like this that you must distance yourself from. FAST. Stop communication. Don't respond to their bait. *No matter what you say, it can and will be used against you.* I read that sentence online referencing narcissists, and it's so true. Narcissists will seek all of your attention and suck up all of your energy, and when you have none left to give or, God forbid, you start questioning them, they will pounce on you or just toss you out like stale garbage. It's sad but true.

Trust me, my love, it is NOT you. It is them.

Please note here that there is a HUGE difference between giving genuine criticism from a place of love and/or seeking to help others see your perspective, versus doing so from a more negative place. Sometimes as the receiver of criticism, it can be hard to digest, but I advise really listening to your body and the way you are feeling after receiving feedback. If you are feeling uncomfortable, that's OK – that signals growth. However, if you are feeling personally attacked as a person, chances are that you are dealing with a hater, and you don't have time for that nonsense. As the incredible Nedra Tawwab states in her book, *Set Boundaries, Find Peace: A Guide to Reclaiming Yourself*, "I spend time around healthy people. I reduce my interactions with people who drain my energy. I protect my energy against people who threaten my sanity."

Sub-Lesson B: Seize every opportunity!

"Don't wait for anyone else to walk into your life and floor you. Do it yourself." – Rebecca Kennedy, *Peloton workout*

As Mark recently reminded me and a wise person once said, *half of the battle is just showing up* (it's mostly attributed to Woody Allen). This means you need to meet with people and take your butt out to where your people are if you are trying to make it anywhere in life. You never know who you might meet! So many of my successes have come to me because I was willing to get out there and talk to people. If I didn't expose myself to new people on a regular basis, I would merely stay stagnant. Who wants that?

Once you meet people, you can utilize their knowledge and take the opportunity to speak up! Let them know your needs and your wants. This is how you get whatever it is you want in life. Sometimes just doing what comes naturally in a setting will get you far.

When I attended the 2019 Women's March in Washington DC, I knew that I was going to be writing an article for a local online publication. I assumed that I would just be reporting on the general atmosphere with a few quips here and there from various attendees. What transpired, however, was so organic and beautiful that I still consider it to be one of my favorite pieces of journalism. I found myself marching with three fabulous women with incredible stories to tell, and I decided that it was my perfect opportunity to tell them. I am still connected with these inspirational women, and by sharing their experiences with me, they became mentors by allowing me to share them with the world.

Utilize the places that you attend regularly – whether it's your gym, place of worship, office, library, your kid's soccer practice, even the grocery store – to have conversations with those around you. Let them know what you do; you never know what benefits you will find. By talking with another mom at my eldest son's karate dojo, I discovered that she managed a woman who could help me design my business logo.

If you are looking for opportunities, be assertive. Offer your time and assistance to others and I assure you will get theirs in return...unless you are insincere, in which case they will be able to smell it from a mile away, and you will suddenly disappear from their list of people that they know they can call for help. No one wants this.

25

Life Lesson #8: Mentors come in all shapes and sizes. Pay attention to them but take only what you need.

"A mentor is someone who allows you to see the hope inside yourself." – Oprah Winfrey, The Internet (I mean, seriously. This quote is all over the damn place but I cannot find the source. Oprah, if you're reading this, I love you, and I'm sorry.)

I have been so fortunate to have mentors in every aspect of my life. We all can, if we just pay attention. You already read about my mentor, Karen, in the hotel industry and Richard in our Everytown Survivor Network (more on him shortly). While these mentors came to me organically, I have also found celebrity mentors while reading and listening to podcasts (Brené Brown, if you ever read this – you are a fucking bold brave goddess in every sense of the word). In our current era of technology with information at our fingertips, why not take advantage of this amazing opportunity to get free advice from people with decades of experience?!

While we have this opportunity to learn from our friends, mentors, and public figures, it's important to remember that what works for them may not work for us. Adapt recommendations that you love, but don't feel like you have to listen to everyone. If it doesn't feel right to you, you don't need to buy into it. You don't have to agree with every self-help book out there. (After all, that's why there are so many.) Hell, you don't have to agree with me. As long as you are following your heart and have an open mind to learning, you are on the right path. Let me give you some examples of where I have found unexpected mentors.

Example 1:

I read the book *To Love and Let Go* by Rachel Brathen, an incredibly talented and loving yoga instructor who has been through some of the worst traumas that anyone can experience – from losing her best friend to a tragic car accident; to her mother repeatedly trying to kill herself; to multiple other deaths and traumas. Her book resonates deeply with my own traumas. Between her book, her yoga teachings, and her posts on Instagram, I feel connected to Rachel even though I have never met her. She feels deeply just as I do. By sharing such a big piece of her heart, she has helped *me* feel my own feelings.

Before I found Rachel on Instagram, a friend actually recommended that I listen to her podcast. That is where she first resonated with me. At the time, she had a new baby, and as a young mom myself, I could relate to much of what she was saying. The mom guilt, the feelings – everything. Little did I know how much I would have in common with this fabulous woman and how much she would inspire me in the coming years to keep being unapologetically me.

Example 2:

Another friend recommended that I listen to Jenna Kutcher's podcast called *The Goal Digger* podcast when I started my Bold Brave Goddess business. She knew that even though Jenna is in an entirely different industry than me, I would find useful information from her. Not only that, but I am constantly in awe of Jenna's ability to deliver an entire podcast without use of the words "um" or "uh." This woman literally sounds like a professional, like she has been publicly speaking for decades. She is also a self care and self-love advocate, unapologetically posting pictures both of her squishy, post-baby body, as well as pictures of her hard-earned fit body. It reminded me that I can love my body just as it is without constantly stressing over weight fluctuations and calorie counting. **We need these constant reminders of what we already know**.

Example 3:

One of my favorite mentors, Richard Martinez, I have already spoken about. My compassion for Richard began from the moment I saw him publicly grieving on TV after his son Christopher was murdered, crying out to legislators that they will never do anything to strengthen our lax gun laws unless they experience the pain that he has. I admired his emotion and his spirit. When I met him at our Moms Demand Action conference years later, after having also seen him in a film (he's been featured in a few for his gun violence prevention work), I felt a little starstruck, but it was also like I was meeting another family member. In fact, when he addressed our survivor group, he said that we indeed are all like family, because we have a special bond and are in a club that no one ever wants to experience or join. Richard later gave copies of his entire speech to those of us privileged to sit at his table for lunch the next day.

When I was accepted into the survivor fellowship program the following year, I was ecstatic that Richard was one of the trainers and that I would have some one-on-one time with him. One valuable thing that I learned from him is to keep things simple. He recommended when giving speeches to use shorter words that everyone can understand, and if you can say things in fewer words, do it. Hearing this gave me a sense of empowerment that I have also applied to my writing. I can't tell you how annoying it is to read books or articles where the authors are so damn pretentious that I feel like I am looking up every other fucking word I read. Seriously, what are they trying to prove? Personally, I think swear words make the best adjectives, and you can rest assured everyone will understand those!

My most intimate moment with Richard came on the 5-year mark of my dad's death. I was invited to help train the new class of survivor fellows in 2019, which I accepted because I was honored to be chosen. This was a big mistake, though, as I was there on the 5-year mark of my dad taking his life. Something told me that I would be OK because I was going to be with a group of people who knew exactly what I was going through. However, I didn't anticipate the way it would hit me that year, in a room full of people discussing their most traumatic moments. I took a break for a while in my hotel room, sobbing and letting myself feel my feelings. When I thought I was feeling better, I returned to the training. As I was walking into the room, Richard reached out to hug me. He gave me a knowing look. It was then that I became a puddle in his arms, and he just held me. This is what it's like to be survivor strong – to be there for one another in our darkest and most grief-filled moments.

Another unforgettable moment with Richard is from the year prior when he was training me to become a survivor fellow. As I sat next to Richard, I told him that I often think of him. He responded by saying that we "should be" thinking of the students in Parkland, as the Marjory Stoneman Douglas High School shooting had just occurred 2 months prior. What I said to him was this: "Your story is just as important." After I said those words to him, he began talking about his son Christopher and telling me about his love of basketball and girls. When I repeated this story to another leader in our Everytown organization, she said, "Wait, you said that to Richard?" That is when I realized that I could also be a mentor to the one who mentors me. I now regularly check in with Richard and make sure that he is taking care of himself. **Never underestimate your own strengths and the power of your words.**

26

Life Lesson #9: Leave time for self care or you will burn the fuck out.

"Caring for myself is not self-indulgence. It is self-preservation, and that is an act of political warfare." – Audre Lorde, *A Burst of Light: And Other Essays*

Right now, I am attempting to do my self care, realizing that I'm feeling the way that I'm feeling because I have such empathy for others and I realize that right now I just need to rest. As much work as I know that needs to be done right now, I also know that my needs come first. The cliché is indeed true that I can't pour from an empty cup. I also have to recognize that some people are equipped to handle more than me, and some are less equipped. It doesn't do me any good to compare myself to these people because their experiences and backgrounds are so different from my own.

Know what your self care is, not just what makes you feel good at the time, but what will ultimately make you feel better in the long run. I know all too well the repercussions and shame that come from short-term feel-good "solutions."

Sub-Lesson A: Saying no to others is saying yes to yourself.

"When you love what you do and amazing opportunities come up that aren't a good fit for you but you're tempted to say yes – have someone you can call to run it by and think through the question – if I say yes to this, what will I be consequently saying no to?" – Jenna Kutcher, *Goal Digger* Blog

There are many versions of the quote, and it has been around for several years. However, when I am preaching self care in meetings and using this quote, I have had folks ask me to repeat it so that they can write it down. *Here is your chance.* Highlight it, write it down, tattoo it on your brain (or hell, even on your skin)!

When I first joined Moms Demand Action and became a Survivor Fellow with Everytown for Gun Safety, I had a hard time turning down any opportunity to volunteer my time or lend my voice. If I didn't have another hard commitment on my calendar for the date and time I was being asked to help, it was an automatic yes. I barely even checked in with my husband to make sure we didn't have other family commitments.

By doing this, not only did I create a rift in my own marriage, but I was over-exerting myself. As my friend and mentor Richard stated to me, I never slowed down to give myself proper rest time. My mom was beginning to worry about me. Little did I know, Mark and my mom were constantly in communication about me and my well-being, both worried that I was going to burn the fuck out.

I did burn out. After planning the March for Our Lives

in 2018 and leaving the following day for our family spring break vacation to Cancun, my intention was to take a break from social media so that I could just enjoy our time together. Unfortunately, I didn't keep my promise to myself because I was too busy trying to keep up-to-date on the videos and pictures that I was being tagged in all over the media for the march and rally. I stayed up at night sitting in our small hotel bathroom, scrolling through my Twitter, Facebook, and news articles so that I wouldn't wake up my kids.

It took me a long time to know my own boundaries and to start saying no. In fact, one of my New Year's intentions in 2019 was to start saying "no" more. I guess you could say that I did, but it wasn't nearly enough. I still found myself with hardly any free time to do things that I love or even just to relax! With each passing year, I am getting much better. I just said no to someone last week, and it felt so damn good. It was something I didn't want to do, so I said no and offered to do something that I love instead. That's a huge win!

Many of us grew up being taught to always say yes to everything. **We must re-train our brains to respond differently.**

Sub-Lesson B: Part of knowing your own boundaries is being able to manage your time effectively.

'When we are in what I refer to as 'crazy busy' mode, we are simply less capable of handling the busy." – Dr. Darria Long, 'How to Triage Your Busy Life" TED Talk

I watched this incredible TED Talk one day while looking for something to occupy myself as I walked on my treadmill. As I subsequently shared the talk with my friends, I informed them it was life-changing for me. Here's why. Dr. Long compares our lives to the emergency room where she works. She states quite plainly that we must prioritize our to-do list as they do in the ER using a color-code. Sounds simple, right? Grocery shopping takes precedence over vacuuming the floor because we need to eat! But what about the e-mails that come rolling in as you are trying to finish a project? Do you respond, or can they wait? I think you know the answer to that question. Since listening to this TED Talk, I have set two main goals for each day as opposed to my former pipe dreams of accomplishing everything in my to-do list. By doing so, I am more purposeful in my actions and don't feel like a fish out of water, flailing and gasping for air because I can't keep up with endless demands on my time.

Not too long ago, I sat across from a friend and said out loud, "I literally don't know where my time goes." However, upon repeating that sentence to Mark, I admitted that yes, I DO know where it goes, but I realized that I was only doing what I wanted to do and not necessarily accomplishing the things that needed to get done (like writing this damn book). In fact, when my friend asked me if I wanted an accountability partner, I looked at her and said NO only because I was afraid she might text me on a day when I am making up a thousand excuses to not sit down at my computer and just do the damn thing. *Sigh.* When you are a self-made entrepreneur and don't have anyone to report to, it's easy to let yourself slip and find other things to do instead of your job! (Note: as soon as I wrote this, I texted my friend back to set up that accountability check in!)

Sub-Lesson C: Always listen to your body.

"I do my hair toss
    Check my nails
    Baby how ya feelin'?
    Feeling good as hell." – Lizzo in "Good As Hell," by Melissa Jefferson (AKA Lizzo) and Eric Frederic

Self care also involves listening to your body – knowing when to start and when to stop, when to push yourself and when to hold back. You must know your own limits in life. Many people will ask things of you, and you have to know where to draw the line. This also ties in with boundaries and being able to say no. It involves taking care of ourselves, both physically and mentally. I am a huge advocate of healthy eating because I know how shitty I feel when I eat too much sugar, processed foods, or things that my body doesn't tolerate (the list seems to grow longer by the day unfortunately). One weekend while our family was vacationing in San Diego, I let myself fall off the bandwagon. I didn't pay attention to what I was ingesting, and I kept telling myself that it was OK because we were on a short vacation. I had just completed a sugar cleanse a couple of weeks prior, so I was ready to eat *all* the sugar! Boy, did I regret that decision. It seriously fucked with my mind, sending me into a spiral of depression and body shaming. Now was that really worth all of those desserts, or could I have just stopped at one? I face this same battle every time I make desserts, too, eating way too much of the batter as well as the finished product, inevitably beating myself up each time and saying that I won't do that again. Oh, and one year on Christmas Eve, I actually ate so much cake and frosting as I was making it that I forced myself to throw up afterward just so I could feel better. *Really Celeste? Way to go.* (Please note here that I do not condone any of these activities, especially the latter. There is help out there if you or your loved ones are concerned with your eating habits.)

My health coach, who helped me realize all of the food intolerances that were increasing my anxiety, asked me what my thought processes were when I was overeating while baking or going into the holidays. The next time I baked, our conversation made me step back and *think* instead of just shoving the chocolate in my face like my dad used to do. He used to eat whole packages of M&Ms in one sitting. No, I'm not talking individual packages of them, or even king-size packages. I am talking about the bags that you use to fill a dispenser or to dump into a bowl to share with company. He would sit there and just try to eat his misery like I do now when my kids are sick or I'm stressed out. Many of us do this, but we know that it doesn't make us feel good, does it?

My point here is that we have to listen to our bodies, to our minds, and not just let temptation take over. We know the right thing to do. We *always* know the right thing to do, yet we make excuses to deviate from it. This is NOT self care. Just as drinking is not self care. I thank my fellow sober women for their movement, people like Holly Whitaker and Laura McKowen for having the courage to speak up. Telling our sober truths isn't easy – we must face our past demons. In doing so, however, we are taking care of ourselves. We are ripping off the band-aid and exposing the hurt and insecurities that we hid with alcohol for so many years. It's a painful process. Much of the time, growth is. **Growth is self care**.

My growth has been the realization that when I want to blast sad music or eat that piece of chocolate because I'm reminded of something traumatic (such as recently coming across an old notebook with my molester teacher's name in it), I quickly run from the chocolate and put on inspiring music instead (hello Lizzo)! I dance around like crazy to get that energy out of me. Or maybe I go for a run or practice my yoga. I practice the self care that is fulfilling *long term*, NOT the "self care" that is harmful and only soothing in that moment. I used to drown myself in chocolate and alcohol. I can't say that I don't still sometimes eat too much chocolate, but at least now I know that the alternative is way better. My hope is that in writing this down, I will feel less and less tempted. I am learning to take care of myself so that I can keep loving myself. After all, **if I can't love myself, then how can I expect anyone else to do so?**

27

Life Lesson #10: Karma, baby.

"We do not need magic to transform our world. We carry all the power we need inside ourselves already. We have the power to imagine better." – J.K. Rowling, *The Benefits of Failure* Harvard Commencement Speech

OK, so I realize that not everyone believes in karma, but hear me out. Karma has unexpectedly appeared in my life a few times, removing any skepticism I once had. The first example is something that I am still ashamed about, as it's an example of me being a total asshole.

Basically, I had a grown-up temper tantrum because I couldn't get what I wanted. I tried to park in a parking lot that was only meant for a restaurant's customers. The manager was standing out in the parking lot ensuring that people like me, who were there for a marathon expo, weren't using up all of her precious parking spaces. She was even watching to ensure that we were going into the restaurant as we said that we would. Not only did I lie to this woman and try to sneak into the expo, but I also reamed her out in the public parking lot after she threatened to have my car towed. She was merely trying to run her business and ensure that she wasn't losing customers, but at the time I was too irritated to think of anything other than myself and my own convenience. Guess what? On my drive home that night, I developed one of the worst ear infections of my life! I went home and tried everything to make it feel better, only to wake up the next morning and schedule the first doctor's appointment I could. The doctor took one look in my ear and told me it was bright red, and it came on out of NOWHERE.

Karma, baby.

My next example of karma is one that still warms my heart. It was just before Christmas one year, and I decided to do some late night (OK, 9 PM is late in my opinion!) holiday shopping at Target. It wasn't until I reached home that I realized that I couldn't find my wallet anywhere. I told Mark that I would have to go back to the store and look for it. I parked in the same spot I had just been in, looking in all of the carts in the corral where I had just returned mine. I proceeded to look through *all* of the corrals in the parking lot, thinking maybe I had just forgotten which one it was. When I couldn't find the wallet, I walked into the store and asked if any employees had seen it. When they told me they hadn't, I left my name and number for them to call me in case they found it.

Dejectedly, I drove home, and Mark and I stayed up until midnight canceling all of my credit cards. I was so mad at myself and bummed out at the same time.

The next day, Mark received a phone call at work from a man who had found my wallet in the cart in the Target parking lot the night before. This amazing man went through my wallet to find some way to get a hold of me, and what he found was a Humane Society card that had Mark's and my name on it, which led the man to search Mark out on Linked In and call his business. How incredible is that?! He met Mark in a parking lot to return the wallet and would not accept anything for it. He said that he didn't return it to the store because he didn't trust them, and he wanted to be sure that I got it. I still have this man's name saved on my phone so that I may one day return the favor.

Now I still don't know exactly what I did to earn this next act of good will, but I can say that I spend most of my days trying to exude positive energy and spread joy. Several years ago, I ordered a small box of goodies for my grandma from Zingerman's Mail Order, and instead she received a large box of nicer (read: expensive) goodies. When I called to report it and ask if we should return what we received, the sweet woman on the phone said, "You must have been nice to someone. Keep it all and enjoy!"

When we focus our energies on lifting other people up and spreading joy, joy is what we will get in return. When we spend our days like an Eeyore, thinking that nothing good will ever happen to us, nothing good ever will! **You cannot attract good karma if all you are giving out is negative energy.**

Sub-Lesson A: There are two different ways to respond to anger. One is healthy; the other will eat you alive if you let it.

"Sometimes you need to scorch everything to the ground and start over. After the burning the soil is richer, and new things can grow." – Celeste Ng, *Little Fires Everywhere*

I have been ruminating on anger a lot lately, after having just read both Dr. Edith Eger's *The Gift* and Rebecca Traister's *Good and Mad: The Revolutionary Power of Women's Anger.* Dr. Eger is a Holocaust survivor and has spent her whole life working through her resentment and justified anger toward her aggressors, and Rebecca Traister is a journalist who has covered numerous scandals for decades, including that of Harvey Weinstein who assaulted her and her colleague back in 1999. Both Dr. Eger and Traister have incredible perspectives and certainly the lived experiences to dole out advice about how to either let go of or harness our anger. At first glance, it might seem that these women are delivering contradictory messages, but I truly believe that they can coexist. We can be really fucking furious but also want to let our anger dissipate at times so that we can be free. It's a constant struggle we face as women and even as a human species.

I have spent years alternating between bubbling anger and meditative peace. In the words of some of my heroines, The Chicks, "I'm not ready to make nice." (By the way, this is a good song to blast and head-bang to if you're pissed. You're welcome.) Some things I will just never get over, and I think that's OK. Learning how to deal with my strong feelings and process them has been a journey. I've learned how to release my anger in a healthy way so that it doesn't eat me alive. For instance, just last night I devoured 2 pints of ice cream while experiencing flashbacks of past abuse, but by this afternoon, I was able to take my aggression out on my treadmill and release some of the leftover tension in a healthy way.

Recognizing our anger is key so that we can determine how to respond to it. Your anger can eat you up inside if you don't learn how to control it; once you learn how to harness it, it can fuel you to make things better in the world. These responses do not exist in a vacuum. Instead, they swim together in a pool. We must exercise our self-control muscles to ensure that the healthier response surfaces the most.

Dr. Eger, while reflecting on the torture that she endured in Auschwitz, figured out a way to cope with her resentment and hatred of her abusers which eventually led her to a sense of peace after many decades. Traister shares that she had the best sex of her life while writing *Good and Mad* because she found the release exhilarating, and she had access to an awesome outlet in which to present her frustrations to the world. Both women were able to work through their past demons and frustration so that it didn't tear up their souls.

Not all of us are so lucky, in either sense. Perhaps we have experienced unresolved trauma, and/or we have even had years to process it but still aren't quite at that place yet where we can feel as peaceful as Dr. Eger (she is a damn saint in my opinion). Or perhaps we don't have the outlets that Traister does as a writer, and we have to keep quiet because of our circumstances. This makes it all the harder to control that horrible feeling eating us up inside. My biggest advice here is to find someone you can trust to talk to and work through some of your big feelings. **Healing requires things to be spoken and shared; keeping our rage to ourselves only makes it fester and grow.**

28

Life Lesson #11: Develop a mantra.

"If not me, who? If not now, when?" –Emma Watson, *HeForShe* Speech (borrowed from Hillel the Elder)

This is something that came about naturally for me when I wrote my speech for the March for Our Lives event in 2018. At the end of my speech, inspired by Emma Watson speaking on behalf of her new gender equality campaign, HeForShe, in front of the United Nations in 2014 (look her speech up, NOW, if you haven't seen it), I added, "**Be Bold, Be Brave, because if you don't do something, who will?**" It quickly became part of every speech that I gave, and it is now my trademark. As you can see, it's also where I developed my business name.

Another mantra of mine reminds me that no matter where I am at in my journey, I am where I need to be. In fact, I created a meme with the powerful message: **You are enough. Yesterday, today, tomorrow – you are exactly where you are supposed to be.** It was developed from yoga - a mantra often said as we are learning and growing in our poses and the instructor tells us that we are exactly where we are supposed to be. I added the beginning to remind myself that on either side of today, there has been and will be a change. **The only way to keep growing is to keep going.**

As Congresswoman Ayanna Pressley said to *InStyle* Magazine, "I am not in Congress to occupy space; I am here to create it. I walk into every room shoulders back, head held high, reminded that I am the manifestation of so many women who have been pursuing justice for generations." This is a wonderful reminder that every second of every day is an opportunity to reassess our visions and our goals. Our positive mantras will give us the pep talk and the confidence we need to keep showing up for ourselves and for others.

Once you develop your mantra, practice saying it in front of the mirror. And while you are there, practice lifting yourself up and saying words of affirmation to yourself as well. It's up to you to keep reassuring yourself. If you don't believe in yourself, who will?

29

Life Lesson #12: Enjoy the present moment.

"If you spend every day wishing for the next to come
  Aged and lifeless is what (Yes!) you'll become." – Jessie J in
"Stand Up," by Jessica Cornish (Jessie J), David Martin, Geoff
Morrow, David C Martin, Karl Gordon, and John Benson

As I type this on January 1, 2021, with my cynicism over New
Year's resolutions and their frequent failure by February, I
realize that I have a beautiful opportunity to reassess my life. I
can gently close my eyes and envision the life I want to live. Not
the one I had yesterday or even two minutes ago. Just right here,
right now. Living in the present moment is a constant goal of
mine, which is so fulfilling when it occurs. To be able to just
sit, and for instance, listen to my beautiful 5-year old's giggles
(one of my favorite noises in the world, along with my mother's
voice, my 8-year-old telling me how much he loves me, and
my husband asking me if I want coffee – love you, babe).

People who are constantly saying that they can't wait for the
day to end make me sad. I mean, don't get me wrong – I have

bad days, too, and I have certainly said this a few times. I'm quite sure we all have. But when those days outweigh the rest of them, it becomes a problem. If we constantly wish ourselves into the future, we are wasting away our present, not even living fully. Before you know it, your life will be over and there won't be a tomorrow. Why not live the shit out of today?!

I am constantly making lists in my head – lists of what I could be or should be doing instead of enjoying the present moment. As I type this in a beautiful, rented condo in Boyne Mountain, MI while I am supposed to be enjoying myself on vacation, my mind is racing with what laundry needs to be done, what homework my eldest son has to do, what books I want to read, what needs to be packed back up to go home, the other list I need to finish making for our next family trip...the lists are endless. My brain just fires on repeat constantly, saying, "How dare you rest right now when you could be organizing or cleaning something. Or at least, *read a book*!" Only when I am sick do I allow myself to just do what my body is craving – to truly rest.

Yet my mindfulness, meditation, and yoga have taught me that to be *truly* happy, one can only live in the present moment. I tell Mark the same thing when he shares worries of the future with me. We never know what tomorrow is going to throw at us, so we might as well just enjoy what we have at the time. (Unless you are getting a foot tattoo of course. If that is the case, absolutely focus on what you will be doing when that shit is done because that pain is no joke.)

Sub-Lesson A: Love each day as if it were your last.

"I never thought, 'Why me?' In fact, I thought, 'Why not me?'"
– Lucy Hone, *3 Secrets of Resilient People* TED Talk

The tragedies in my life have cemented this lesson into my brain. After experiencing tragedy after tragedy, I know how fragile life can be and how quickly it can end. I used to naively think that nothing bad could happen to me. I remember always lying down in the backseat of my grandparents' huge boat of a Buick, taking long naps with no seatbelt on because it was more comfortable that way, thinking that my grandpa was such a good driver that nothing could ever happen. I thought I would always be OK. Sometimes I long to be in that young, naïve state of mind again. *Why do death and tragedy have to ruin our sense of everything whole and sane and calm?*

It is a shame that it takes tragedy to strike for us to realize this lesson. Unfortunately, I experienced death for the first time when I was merely 18 years old. So many children experience it even younger than that, I know. When I was 18, one of my mom's best friends lost her second daughter, Stefanie, in a tragic car accident at the tender age of 16. Ironically, I had been in a horrible car accident with a semi-truck (it sounds worse than it was) just a year prior. I was so hysterical at the scene, completely unscathed, yet crying that my mom was going to kill me for destroying her car. It turns out, she was just grateful that I was OK. If only the same had been true for her friend's daughter the following year.

That tragic funeral would only be the beginning of a series of funerals that I would attend for souls taken much too young.

131

My friend Carrie Noble died at age 34 from cancer, leaving two small children behind. I think of Carrie almost every day and how unfair it was that she was taken so young. I think of my cousins Ian and Evan, who both died from tragic motor accidents as well. One was newly engaged to be married with so much life ahead of him. The other lived on for several years as a quadriplegic, experiencing many complications and misery. Both young men were in their early 20s when the accidents occurred.

Life is so fucking fragile y'all. Much of the work that I do with Moms Demand Action reminds me of this, too. So many dear friends of mine have holes in their hearts where their children's spirits now live, their bodies taken from this world by the cruelty of a gun. My friend Stephanie's daughter, Dayla, was hit with a stray bullet at age 4. Stephanie's story has touched the hearts of many politicians and TV personalities. When Stephanie did a TV interview on CNN, she held the box with Dayla's ashes in it to show what it's like to lose a child to gun violence. She uses her voice now for the greater good, speaking Dayla's name and making a positive difference in the world – changing hearts and minds, being a total badass. I have been so touched by Stephanie and Dayla's story that I now have a sunflower tattoo on my leg, as a sunflower was the last picture that Dayla drew before she died. Stephanie too has a gorgeous sunflower collage on her arm in Dayla's memory.

I am adding in this paragraph right now in the midst of the coronavirus crisis. This beast of a virus is already going down in history for its unprecedented death rate and the high transmission levels. In the first month of the pandemic, my parents lost a dear friend and a distinguished war veteran to the virus. My heart just absolutely breaks for them and for everyone who knew this amazing man. Too many of our loved ones are being taken from us these days. We must continue to check in with them and tell them how much they mean to us. None of us are immortal. We are all just as susceptible to death as anyone else. *Let's at least love the crap out of each other while we are here.*

One thing that everyone is talking about during the coronavirus crisis is how much goodness and kindness is coming out of this mess. *Why does it take tragedy for us to wake the fuck up and realize how fragile life is?* Unfortunately for me, and for many others who have experienced loss, we already know this. I doubt that anyone living through these tumultuous times - the pandemic, climate change and wildfires, recent and current wars, ongoing tragedies and oppression - will leave this world unscathed or unaffected.

With this said, I have learned always to hug longer than I think I should. I read once that a person can't even experience the healing aspects of a hug unless they hold on for at least 20 seconds. These quick, pat-on-the-back hugs that we often give one another are essentially useless. They don't hold the love in them that long embraces do. After all, when someone is hurting, we hold them in our arms and squeeze them, right? We don't just give them an emotionless pat and send them on their way! We stay with them to show them how much we care. Let's do this every time we hug others, for it's never a guarantee that we will see them again.

Sub-Lesson B: Life is too short to do shit you don't like.

"I just do what lights me up. If I don't feel good about something, I'm not doing it." – Tiffany Haddish, "Tiffany Haddish Shaved Her Head and Fell in Love," *InStyle*

Of course y'all know there is always shit that you absolutely gotta do, even though you hate it. Even if you are financially blessed and don't have to clean your own bathrooms (good for you!), chances are you still have to grit your teeth and sit through boring meetings which you'd rather not attend. What I am instead referencing here are the things for which you have a *choice*.

I overheard someone saying at my gym that they don't have time to read books that don't immediately interest them! While I said AMEN in agreement, it dawned on me that, at the time, I had approximately 8 books stacked up on my side of the bed, a few of which I had started and wasn't thrilled with. They were keeping me from books I hadn't even opened yet but deeply wanted to read. This taught me to prioritize my shit properly!

Sigh.

You all probably realize by now that I am writing this book more for me than for anybody else, right? Because I need to keep listening to my own advice. Don't worry – that's my last life lesson.

Back to where I was originally going with this...life is too short to keep doing things that aren't serving you. Granted, I realize that I come at this from a place of privilege and that I don't have a job I am forced to work just to make ends meet. (If that is the case, you do what you gotta do.) But for those things that we have choices about, by all means, stand up for yourself, your values, and your passions. Do things that inspire you and make you all tingly inside, not things that make your stomach crawl and give you ulcers.

When I first began going to the gym over 14 years ago (how time flies), it took me a while to find my groove. Mark, who was my boyfriend at the time, kept trying to convince me to come to the gym with him. I would be so envious every time we would speak on the phone at night and he would say, "OK, I'm gonna go hit the gym now." I was jealous of his motivation and determination. What I didn't realize is that I have the same, if not more, amount of determination that he does; I just hadn't found the right fit for me. Up until this point, I hadn't explored all of my fitness options. Attempting to do the same yoga or Pilates DVD workout every week wasn't vibing with me. It didn't motivate or inspire me.

As I mentioned in the first part of the book, it all started with a hip hop class at Mark's former gym. I loved the instructor and the music and the moves, and it started me on my journey. Oftentimes, it just takes one thing that can hook us and then we take off – we discover what we *are* good at and then we excel.

I also spoke earlier about my experience with Moms Demand Action and my transition from data to events. I found a way to get out of doing that thing I didn't like (although I will say that having that background and knowledge of our system has come in quite handy as I do my other work). We never know how the journey is going to lead us, but again, we are exactly where we are supposed to be in that moment. We should never doubt our journey even when life is difficult. Even my gun violence survivor friends who have been shot hate the phrase "in the wrong place at the wrong time," because what is the right place to be shot? How does that even make sense?

With this said, I have to add that we mustn't beat ourselves up over our aversions. What others lack, we make up for with our talents and vice versa. We can't excel at EVERYTHING. OK, maybe if you are Lady Gaga, you can. But everyone else, nope. Just focus on what inspires YOU!

Keep on keeping on and doing what you love, friends. You won't regret it.

Sub-Lesson C: Stop dwelling on the past and focus on what you have control over.

"How is it that the world keeps going, breathing in and out unchanged, while in my soul there is a permanent scattering?" – Chimamanda Ngozi Adichie, *Notes on Grief*

Even if your past WAS your fault and you made some shitty decisions (hey, we all do), what exactly is dwelling upon the past and reliving every mistake that you made going to do for you? It's going to keep dragging you deeper and deeper – that's what it's going to do. It's going to pull you down into a quicksand of negativity of which you will have a hard time digging yourself out. You will be a prisoner of your own doing.

When we focus on the negativity of our mistakes, we can't move forward. However, if we focus on the positive aspects of our mistakes – if we see them as an opportunity to grow and learn from, we can help ourselves, and perhaps in doing so, help others. The reason why I share so many of my mistakes while writing is because I know that I am not alone. Again, I have been in this world long enough to know that I am not the first, nor will I be the last, to experience this crazy rollercoaster of life. We all make mistakes. It's up to us to own up to them and to move on.

A friend once commented to a group of us that she "doesn't deserve" for us to validate her or to comfort her. How could any of us not deserve to be forgiven or loved? If we are taking the initiative to make changes in our lives – not just making empty promises, but actively showing our own change and growth – how could we not accept ourselves and let others do the same? We are making these positive changes for a reason. We are becoming better versions of ourselves. We deserve all the love and congratulations and praise. No exceptions.

That said, my body still sometimes craves those nostalgic pulls – those intense feelings of remorse or guilt for past relationship or business failures. This is known as self-sabotage. However, I must remind myself that these were not "failures" but instead **learning opportunities**. I wouldn't be where I am today had it not been for those hard times that I survived. I recently heard the phrase, "Don't gaslight yourself," from a conference speaker. This resonated with me and has encouraged me to shut my mind up when it begins going down those dangerous roads.

When I was recently commiserating to another friend of mine about a series of bad decisions that I made, she said to me, "Your past doesn't define you." Hearing her speak those words to me was so empowering. I have heard it before. In fact, I have heard many of these life lessons and inspirational quotes before, but it doesn't stop me from beating myself up and questioning my decisions. Sometimes we just need that reminder from our friends that we are all human. It's OK to make mistakes. *It's OK to not be OK.* But it's not OK to keep making the same mistakes over and over again. As the wise Maya Angelou said, "When you know better, you DO better." Don't keep fucking up and looking over your shoulder thinking that you can blame someone else for your own unwillingness to face your demons. Yes, it's hard, but it's worth it in the long run. It changes you. It makes you a better person.

30

Life Lesson #13: Change isn't comfortable. It's not supposed to be.

"The first problem for all of us, men and women, is not to learn, but to unlearn." – Gloria Steinem, "A New Egalitarian Life Style," *The New York Times*

This is just like those inspirational fitness posters you see at schools and gyms that say, "Change begins at the end of your comfort zone." It's so true. I equate all of the personal growth I experience in my daily life to the growth I gain at the gym or my yoga practice when I am uncomfortable. The longer I hold poses and feel that sense of discomfort, the more flexibility and strength I gain. If I kept working out in my comfort zone, I wouldn't have the muscle tone that I do. I wouldn't be able to run longer distances or hold warrior poses in yoga.

In life, when we stay in our comfort zones, we aren't taking chances. If I had stayed in my comfort zone, I never would have become a Survivor Fellow with Everytown. I never would have spoken in front of a crowd. I would have kept saying no. Instead, I found something I was passionate about, and I used it as an opportunity. Many of my friends who are active in the gun violence prevention movement say that they wish that they had been more vocal before tragedy struck their homes. They wish that they had used their voices sooner. But now that they are a part of something so big, there is no stopping them.

If you want that raise, if you want that promotion, you have to do things to get there! Maybe you have a hard time asking for things. Maybe you have to do work that is more of a stretch for you; you have to do more training or think harder to accomplish the task at hand. This will all be so worth it though when you see that paycheck, or you get that manager position! **Everything hard was accomplished through discomfort. Growth takes patience.**

Also, when you realize that you were wrong about something, there is no need to cover it up or freak out about it. Just accept it and move on. Once I announced to a room full of Moms Demand Action volunteers that I thought we were all extroverts because of the work that we do. Not only was I quickly shut down and corrected, but I later realized that I have introvert tendencies too (a happily self-proclaimed ambivert). At the time, I felt like an idiot because I had stuck my foot in my mouth, but fortunately later that night, I sat at the dinner table with the leader of the session I was in and apologized, and she told me that she thought I recovered nicely. We are *always* harder on ourselves, so it's nice to hear this kind of feedback. However, you better believe that I took this lesson and used my own embarrassment and discomfort to prevent myself from making a similar mistake again! ALL of us have to work on our inner selves – that is something we can never escape from, and it shows our true character so much more than our shell of a body.

My wise therapist friend posted on social media about the

importance of loving your partner for their inner beauty, as that is what truly defines them. Sometimes we get so caught up in our outer beauty that we forget to work on our internal battles. I was so damn guilty of this myself. I worked out so fucking hard, thinking only of my toned body, but ignoring the fact that inside I was unhappy. I was angry, depressed, and anxious. Until I came to grips with this, I couldn't improve. Until I was able to face my own discomfort in my path to self-improvement, I couldn't get anywhere. **Inner growth is *much* more uncomfortable than outer growth.**

Sub-Lesson A: Stop being a damn robot and saying what you think it is you're supposed to say.

"Those who are brave enough to be authentic and real, in an era where we are taught to fake it until we make it, are really the world-changers in our society." – Zoë Clark Coates, *Beyond Goodbye*

Instead of apologizing when someone tells us something tragic or sad, let's try to be more helpful. In the words of my dear survivor sister Dr. Doreen Dodgen-Magee, we can say, "I am feeling so much compassion for you right now." I mean, what am I supposed to say when someone tells me that they are sorry that my dad killed himself? "It's OK?" Because it's not. It's absolutely not OK. But it's apparently my job to tell you that it's OK so you can stop feeling bad for me. NO. Let's really say what we mean and what is helpful rather than what has been practiced for God knows how long and became a horrible go-to when we were at a loss for words.

Sometimes there are no words to say.

Sometimes we can just sit with our discomfort as we support our friends and loved ones. This lets them know that we can truly feel what they are feeling, demonstrating empathy instead of sympathy.

Sub-Lesson B: Lean into the discomfort.

"We have to be visible. We should not be ashamed of who we are." – Sylvia Rivera, "Queens in Exile: The Forgotten Ones" Essay

This may sound a little repetitive, but I have an example I want to share. When my husband and I are having a difficult conversation, my initial reaction is either to zone out or to start cussing him out in my head (the typical fight or flight that we learned all about in the book we read together called *Hold Me Tight* by Dr. Sue Johnson). Instead, I remind myself to take a deep breath and just listen, to take everything in and lean into my uncomfortable feelings. What does it actually mean to "*lean in*?" It means to stop putting your guards up and stop building walls when you feel uncomfortable. Let yourself feel those yucky feelings! I promise you – they get better in time. Your body becomes accustomed to the discomfort. Hard conversations will never become easy, but with practice, they become more manageable. I always feel better once everything is said and done. **Discomfort = growth, every damn time.**

Sub-Lesson C: Focus on changing yourself, not blaming others.

"...in these dark times, we not only have the ability to find the light, but I feel like we have the ability to BE the light – to dig down within ourselves and find a way to make the world better."
– Kristin Harmel, to *Costco Connection*

If all we do is place blame on other people and situations for bad things that have happened in our lives, we won't make it far. Everyone will know us for our negative energy. My grandma Smith was the epitome of this – full of blame and resentment and bitterness, something that she passed on to her children. It's no wonder my dad was so fucked up. His own mother never believed anything was her fault. She didn't want to take credit for the pain and the hurt built up inside of her.

We all know people who have this mentality. I picture them in a tornado of their own making, like the character Pig-Pen from Charlie Brown – except instead of a cloud of dirt, they are surrounded in a cloud of negativity, resentment, and blame. They have dug themselves a hole so deep that it's nearly impossible to climb out. Instead of focusing on what they could be doing to better themselves or to change their situation, they just place blame on everyone else. Nothing is ever their fault. Everything is a sob story.

There comes a point where we must get up and take responsibility for our own lives and stop wanting to be the exception to everything as an excuse to get out of doing the actual work we need to do. Here I am speaking from personal experience because I used to be the kid in high school who wanted to challenge all of my teachers when they would make a statement or create an assignment. I would have a personal rebuttal as to why their lecture or assignment did not apply to me. At best, I sounded like an annoying know-it-all. At worst, I was losing friends because I was wasting everyone's time when I could have either, A) spoken to the teacher privately instead of using precious class time, or B) accepted that I didn't have to comment on everything or make everything about me. This is something that I still need to remind myself now and then, being as outspoken as I am.

To move forward, we must take responsibility for the stupid shit we have done and continue to do, but then MOVE the fuck on. Say to yourself, "Damn, that was really fucking stupid," but don't sit there in your own pity party. **Just because bad things happened to us in our past doesn't give us permission to sit quietly and let bad things continue to happen to us.**

You have to fix yourself before you can focus on other people. I spent so many years trying to place blame on others, not recognizing my own faults and shortcomings. I wasn't ready to dig deep into the reasons for my actions, but I had to stop pointing my finger at others for my own hurt. Because I was traumatized in childhood, I constantly subconsciously searched for ways to re-traumatize myself. When I had this realization, I was finally able to set up a healthy boundary for myself, agreeing to no longer allow drama and toxicity in my life.

It's common to use others as your scapegoat, but where does that leave you? Lonely and in the same predicament as you always were. *How about let's focus on your own faults and anger and grudges, Celeste?* I am not saying that I have mastered this. Hell, I can't even say how far I've come. On bad days, I feel like I am drowning in my own resentment, but on good days, I can hold my head proudly and say, "Hell, I've made it this far. Why not keep going?"

31

Life Lesson #14: Be unapologetically you.

"Arms out wide, claim your space." - Megan Rapinoe, *One Life*

This lesson ties in so well with many of the other life lessons, but I wanted to separate it so that it stands out. First of all, it applies directly to my feelings about my writing in this moment. Last night, as I sat across from my husband at a Valentine's Day dinner (yes, we miraculously found an available babysitter on V-Day – score!), I vented to him about my frustrations with my book. As I sit here writing, I find myself picking my own words apart, criticizing the flow of my book, and even questioning the format. I have read several self-help and inspirational books, and each time I do, I compare the layout and the way that the book was written with the way that I am writing mine. Mine is too *different*.... As I said this out-loud to my husband last night, I realized how ridiculous I sounded. He said, "You've never been afraid to be different before!" I laughed and suddenly my stress dissipated. I decided to just keep writing and being me.

For years I would clam up and feel like I had to fit a certain mold if people complimented me or told me that I inspired them. Suddenly I felt this pressure to keep doing exactly what they complimented me on in order to be that same inspiring person – *who they wanted me to be*. After years of living this soul-crushing life, I finally realized that if I just kept being ME, nothing else mattered. What matters most is that I am true to *myself*. If I am against something now that I was all about 4 years ago, it just means that I have *grown*. I have changed my ways. I don't need to keep myself in this small box to adhere to the values that others see in me. It only makes me feel small, or "caged" as Glennon Doyle says. It was Glennon's book, *Untamed*, that led me to this epiphany. Now I know that if I just keep being my badass self, I will not only be free and happy, but I will also thrive. And in thriving, I can continue inspiring.

In the book *The Subtle Art of Not Giving a Fuck* by Mark Manson, it's refreshing to hear his perspective on how <u>not caring</u> as much can actually lead to success. We spend so much time trying to be the perfect person for everyone, but by just being ourselves and not worrying what others think of us or what the outcome will be, it actually gives us the freedom and flexibility to achieve **more**. What a concept!

As aforementioned in Lesson #1, we often put our heroes/-mentors/idols up on pedestals. Then when they say something that doesn't align with who we thought they were, they come crashing down. Let's not put that kind of pressure on them to be what we narrowly perceive of them. I have had to really work on my self-conscious mindset that naturally occurs after someone tells me that I am their hero. *No pressure, right?* **We are not what others think we are.** We don't need to live up to some preconceived notion of how we think others see us. All we can do is continue to be unapologetically ourselves, and in doing so, we won't let ourselves down.

This is why I frequently use the hashtag #unapologeticallyme on Instagram. Do I care if I have makeup on in every post? Nope. Do I care if I expose my innermost feelings to the world? Hell no. Because I know that I am not alone. I have lived enough, read enough true stories, and spoken to so many friends and strangers to know that while my story is uniquely my own, it runs parallel to many others. By speaking my truth and not obsessing over the outcome of doing so, I gain so much confidence. Always be unapologetically you. **What other people think about you is none of your business!**

Sub-Lesson A: Don't lessen who you are to please others.

"Any definition that limits you is inherently flawed." – María de la Soledad Teresa O'Brien, in "Black / Latina," from *One Drop: Shifting the Lens on Race*, arranged by Dr. Yaba Blay

As many of my life lessons are, it's cliche but true: True friends will love you and accept you no matter what. You must be your own true authentic self if you want to feel comfortable in your own skin. You have to live with yourself for the rest of your life. Everyone else gets to choose that option, but **you** don't.

As women, we censor ourselves far too often. We fear we are too much. We are not our true authentic selves. What a shame that we live so much of our lives trying to fit into a mold of what other people think of us. Shouldn't what **we** think of ourselves be more important? Do we really want to keep letting ourselves down for the rest of our lives?

The other day, Mark thought he would embarrass me by yelling out as I was gardening that Spanx® were on sale. I lifted my shoulders up, head held high, and said I am proud of the fact that I wear Spanx® because they make me look good. While it may seem that this is "lessening" myself, in my opinion, it's only amplifying and advocating for myself and what makes me look and feel good.

Sub-Lesson B: Do what makes you feel confident, not necessarily what you are "supposed" to do.

"...I waited a while for

A moment to say I don't owe you a goddamn thing." – Halsey, "Nightmare," by Ashley Frangipane (AKA Halsey), Benjamin Levin, Magnus August Høiberg, Elena Kiper, Nathan Perez, Ivan Shapovalov, Martin Kierszenbaum, Sergey Sasunikovich Galoyan, Trevor Horn, and Valery Polienko

Something that I am constantly in awe of is talented people who can deliver a speech completely unscripted with no preparation. To them, this is just who they are, and it is a natural talent. Just like I was gifted with being able to sit down and write, these folks are able to get up and speak. While I wish that I had this talent (who doesn't?), I know that for me to give a good speech, I have to prepare for it, and I have to have it written down. I get nervous and I know that I would totally draw a blank if I didn't have the words in front of me.

For a while, I let this bother me. I kept asking myself why I wasn't good enough to give a speech off the cuff. Why couldn't I get up in front of a crowd and bring them to their feet with words that just came to me as I was saying them? I watched in awe while others did this within the gun violence prevention community, and it pained me that I was not capable of this.

Then, I studied other speakers, both in the gun violence prevention community and in politics. I watched as people that I loved and respected read from a piece of paper or a prompter. Suddenly I didn't feel so inadequate because I wasn't doing what I thought I was "supposed" to be doing. **There are many different ways of doing the same thing.** Many times, there is no right or wrong way – simply different ways. I also learned that the people who are so incredibly gifted with delivering speeches from the heart with no prompt will often say that they are incapable of giving scripted speeches. We all have our talents and can embrace them for what they are. After all, I am just grateful that now I am able to get up in front of a large crowd and speak, considering it's something that brought me to my knees just a handful of years ago. I have come such a long way, and I need to celebrate and focus on <u>that</u>, NOT on my shortcomings.

Sub-Lesson C: Stop comparing yourself to others. You are not other people!

"Never be ashamed of what you feel. You have the right to feel any emotion that you want, and to do what makes you happy." – Demi Lovato, "Exclusive Interview: Demi Lovato," *Seventeen*

Comparison quotes date back to the Bible in Romans, warning against trying to be something that we are not just because we see it in someone else. I spent way too much of my childhood and early adult life longing to be other people or to have another person's body. It wasn't until I reached my mid-thirties and started forming such a strong appreciation for my body that I was finally able to let go and just live my own life. It can be a constant challenge seeing what everyone else is doing and how flawless others look, but in our social media era, we must remember that so many filters exist. We tend to put only our best face forward online. And even in person, just because someone looks flawless on the outside, we never know what internal demons they are battling. One of my favorite poignant poems demonstrates this all too well; it is called "Richard Cory" by Edwin Arlington Robinson. The poem begins by describing Richard Cory as a handsome, well-spoken man whom everyone thought was so composed, only to end the poem with Richard Cory taking his own life with a gun. These battles we face as humans are extreme, and this is a perfect example of why we must not compare our lives with the lives of others. I remind you; **everything is not always as it seems**.

How often do we scroll through social media and compare ourselves to what others are doing and say that we aren't doing enough? Especially when you are politically involved, or are a mom, or own a business, or hell, do *anything* really – yes, I suppose it applies to everyone. Just stop it already with the comparisons. Stop saying, "Well, I only made 25 phone calls, not 500 like Veronica." Or "I merely did a 30-minute workout, not a full hour." Or the worst, in my opinion, "I am not nearly as good a mom as Leslie, from everything I see that she posts on her Instagram." It's been said before, but I will repeat it here – people mostly only post their happiest moments and lovely lives, NOT the shitstorms that take place behind closed doors. Mind you, there are people out there like me who try to expose reality – who show what it's like to live in the pains of anxiety, or what a pain in the ass it is to live in the middle of a pandemic with two young boys; but those posts are few and far between, interspersed between perfectly toned abs, inspiring stories and wins, and lovely family portraits with smiling kids and arms wrapped around each other like a damn Lifetime movie.

It's also important to remember that *success looks different for everyone*. One of my pet peeves is when someone says, "I'm a slow runner." Listen, I don't care if you run a 6-minute mile or a 12-minute mile. What matters is YOUR progress. What matters is what YOU are accomplishing. As long as you are moving forward, then you are in the right place. You are exactly where you are supposed to be, right now.

Of course, the caveat to this is that sports (and many other games and activities) would not exist if HEALTHY competition did not exist. So if you are Desiree Linden, of COURSE you are going to be comparing your marathon timing with Shalane Flanagan. By the way, in case you don't follow women's running, you should know that badass Des Linden kindly waited for Shalane Flanagan to use the porta potty while running in the Boston marathon so that she could pace her back into the main group, after which Desi proceeded to win the whole damn race. Yet another example of good karma!

Sub-Lesson D: There is no such thing as perfection!

"It's time to start liking who the fuck you are." – Leslie Jones, "Ready for Prime Time," *The New Yorker*

While listening to a podcast about Martin Luther King Jr. and hearing his inspiring words in his "I Have a Dream" speech, I felt my mouth uttering the words alongside him as tears flowed from my eyes. Toward the end of the podcast, the narrator said that Dr. King was not perfect, but no man is. Hearing this, I found myself wondering why we as humans even use this terminology. It's such a cliché and it is so obvious. So why do we even utter these words? Why do we say, "They are not perfect, BUT....?" *I mean seriously.* Can we just stop with this already?

Who defines perfection anyway? I'm starting to even hate the word "perfect." I am convinced that nothing is perfect because it will surely evolve anyway. I just did a quick search online, "pursuit of perfection," after hearing my husband repeat this phrase as I type this; so many articles, speeches, and books popped up. If this is something that we are all in agreement is an unhealthy goal, let's all do better to remove it from our vocabulary. Remember that sage quote from Roxane Gay in Sub-Lesson A in my very first lesson? When we expect perfection and put ourselves or others on pedestals, we are bound to be disappointed.

Now a couple of months later, I am adding to this piece about perfection after listening to my husband scold me because he thought I was spending way too much time on a PowerPoint presentation. And I get it. I truly do. The time that I spend focusing on every minute detail – every slide, every picture, every speaker's note – takes precious time away from my family when I'm working on said presentation at night which I have been for the past few days. It was a wakeup call for me to just focus and let things be. After reviewing my presentation for the fourth time, I realized it was time to call it done.

Mark says that he tells his coworkers this too – that if they focus on the unimportant details such as the color of the screen, they lose the big picture. He said, "At the end of the day, if the background is reddish orange instead of reddish pink, it will be OK." (However, I am skeptical, as Mark is colorblind. Details, details...)

Sub-Lesson E: Your worth is not determined by how many followers you have. Stop obsessing about it!

"Your life cannot be about not upsetting people." – Brit Barron, *Worth It*

As I previously discussed in Life Lesson #4, when I first began my Bold Brave Goddess Instagram account, I wanted a certain number of followers. I thought I immediately needed a large following to feel validated. I quickly realized that when I tried to gain followers the easy way (by paying for it and then merely having a bunch of fake bot followers that I had to report individually and delete) that it just wasn't worth it. Success is only gained through hard work. By continuing to post my honest and vulnerable content, I slowly gain followers. It's much more rewarding that way. Don't put so much pressure on yourself to gain/maintain a certain number of followers, because in the end, those **numbers don't matter and do not determine your true worth**.

32

Life Lesson #15: Sometimes we just need to say things aloud in order to come to our own epiphanies.

"People can tell you to shut up, but they can't keep you from having an opinion. You can't forbid someone to have an opinion, no matter how young they are!" – Anne Frank, *The Diary of a Young Girl*

Often I can solve my own problem that has been cycling in my head for hours or days by speaking it out loud to a family member (usually my mom) or a friend. By speaking our truth and verbalizing our frustrations, we can usually come up with our own solutions. This is the core on which therapy is based. The therapist is there to help you work through things by being an ear and asking questions, NOT by giving you all the answers. After all, **we are the only ones who can make positive changes in our lives**. No one can force us. We must have the courage and determination to do so ourselves.

It helps to talk through your emotions and your hard times. I often create Instagram or Facebook Lives because I know that if I am going through a hard time, it is likely that someone else is as well. In fact, the one that I created this morning elicited a response from one of my dear friends who also struggles with depression and anxiety. She said that I said the words that she needed to hear. You can totally make someone's day just by speaking your truth.

In the same way, you can uncover your innermost feelings by setting free your immediate response to something via your mouth (or your fingers if you are typing). Granted, knee-jerk reactions can come back to bite us as they certainly have me countless times, but they have also opened doors for me or helped me express something that I had been holding inside. One such thing happened when I responded to a friend who said that she "stalked" my Facebook. This caused an unexpected visceral reaction in my body, so I typed her back, telling her I am not too keen on that phrase. I honestly told her that I have used the term "stalk" myself when referencing merely looking at friends' social media accounts, even though I am all too familiar with the true meaning of the term "stalk" and the terror it can cause. It was an epiphany to me to stop using the term if it was eliciting such a visceral response in me when others said it.

Sub-Lesson A: When wisdom and inspiration come to you, write that shit down!

"Our thoughts become our words, our words become our beliefs, our beliefs become our actions, our actions become our habits, and our habits become our realities." – Jen Sincero, *YOU are a BADASS*

I'm currently beating myself up for the ideas that have come to me over the last month (while in coronavirus quarantine) that I haven't taken the time to write down. It's really frustrating and annoying because my inspiration inevitably comes to me when I am in the shower, driving, or right before bed. Not exactly conducive to writing shit down.

So, what do I do? Well, I *try* to use my phone for my notes since I pretty much always have it on me (well, except when I am searching for it, which consumes way too much of my life). I write most of my speeches and poems in my phone notes. I have a huge note in my phone with ideas for this book (and now for book #2 as well). I also like to pull my phone out when people are giving me advice or recommendations on what to read or where to go – I have lists for those too. Lastly, I have been a quote collector since I can remember, and I write or type them every chance I get – many times they have inspired me to come up with my own quotes or stories.

Since I am constantly using my phone as a writing tool, I have been told to use my voice to text to give my poor thumbs a break. In fact, I think I am getting arthritis from all the damn texting I do. Note to self: start speaking into my phone more, for notes and just in general. My body will thank me later.

33

Life Lesson #16: Grief is not linear.

"Grief makes me heavy. It makes me slow. Even on days when I laugh a lot, or dance, or finish a project, or meet a deadline, or celebrate, or make love, it is there." – Ann Hood, *Comfort: A Journey Through Grief*

I gave an interview for our Everytown for Gun Safety *Moments that Survive* website, where we honor and remember survivors and victims of gun violence in the month of February. The reason that we do this is that we have more gun deaths by the end of January in our country than any other industrialized nation has in their *entire calendar year*. So yes, we want to shine a light on our crisis and amplify our survivor voices. When I was interviewed, I spoke of the grief that I feel, and how it just hits me out of nowhere. As my survivor friend Regina Thomson-Jenkins states in her book *After the Storm: Our Journey Through Grief*, "The process of grief can be devastating for anyone going through the different stages. No one experiences the stages of grief in any particular order. There are no rules governing the process of mourning. It's quite similar to being on a roller coaster. Emotions can and will flare at any moment, and there's nothing you can do to stop the tears."

Trauma can be compared to a fresh piercing (though, obviously on a much larger scale). The swelling, redness, and irritation I experienced after my Monroe piercing was slightly reminiscent of the non-linear grief I have endured since my father's suicide. It's a shock to the system at first. It's a sharp jab that brings you down, but then you adjust.... Later your body swells up, similar to the effects of the trauma. You remain swollen for a while until the healing process begins. Sometimes you may have the occasional swelling/pain that comes out of nowhere. Something hits you the wrong way (like my youngest son elbowing me right in my freshly pierced lip), and it's like you are back to square one. With trauma, it is often a smell, as so much of our brain and our memories are connected to scents. For me it was also hearing my uncle speak after my father passed away, as their voices were almost identical. (Unfortunately, my uncle later passed away from cancer, which activated a whole new level of grief.)

In these moments, we must be present with what we are feeling. We must be kind to ourselves. We must reach out for help when we need it. And when we are feeling OK and we see that others are struggling, we do the same for them. Life is such a fucking journey, and we have to hold on to our seats or we may just get flung off the rollercoaster of emotion that life brings us. Cling to your friends and your loved ones, for you never know what tomorrow brings.

In the grief process, you will periodically confront new details that reopen your wounds. For instance, as I was researching information about my dad's family for the beginning of this book, I stumbled upon a personal protection order that my ex-stepmom had filed against my dad. The modified PPO allowed my dad to possess or purchase a firearm. *It is difficult even to type as I continue to process this.* What this means is that my ex-stepmom had felt strongly enough to run away from my dad and file a PPO against him...exactly the type of person who should not be anywhere near a firearm...yet somehow my dad talked her into letting him keep his shotgun anyway, which he eventually used to take his own life.

So now I am processing this whole new level of grief and fucked-up-ness. On the one hand, I am aware that my dad was abusive and had a negative impact on my life for many years, but on the other hand, I still struggle with the concept that my dad killed himself. In accordance with this life lesson, it will undoubtedly be something that I process and grieve over for the rest of my life.

There is strength in being vulnerable and feeling shitty but soldiering on.

To add to the grief of my dad's sudden death, as I was in the final stages of editing this book, my stepdad had a massive, fatal heart attack. His death made me process and analyze our entire relationship. During this process, I decided to check out four separate grief support books from our local library. My favorite is called Beyond Goodbye *by Zoë Clark-Coates. Clark-Coates expounds upon the fact that when experiencing grief, you are unexpectedly taken upon a journey through your past, evaluating your life and perhaps re-traumatizing yourself with former losses. My favorite quote in* Beyond Goodbye *reverberates so much into my soul that I incorporated its concept into a tattoo to honor my stepdad (even though he hated tattoos...sorry Dad!). She says, "The love I carry for you makes me braver, for now I carry your sword*

160

and mine."

34

Life Lesson #17: No matter how much we think we know, we still have so much to learn from others.

"Amazing the things you find when you bother to search for them." – Sacagawea, Source Unknown (Perhaps she said it to Lewis and Clark, who would have been lost without her navigation and communication skills.)

Several years ago on *Ellen*, I watched as she interviewed Tom Hanks for his amazing portrayal of Mr. Rogers. In this interview, Tom Hanks said that, rather than immediately sharing his vast wisdom with others, he has an acronym he uses that is called WAIT, which stands for "Why am I talking?" This is such a great rule to live by, and certainly not one I have always followed.

In fact, I often think that I am better with texting or e-mailing people versus talking in person or over the phone (although I am still old fashioned and much *prefer* talking). This is because I have time to process my thoughts and really think before responding. I don't get to be as impulsive when I actually have to spell out the words versus just letting them flow out of my mouth uncensored.

Think about to whom you are talking. No matter what position they are in, in relation to you, I guarantee that the wisdom and the words that they have to offer could teach you something. Even if it is a child, let their innocence and their beautiful view of the world take you on a ride; bask in their playful approach to life. We often discount children for their contributions, but let me tell you, I have learned more shit from my kids than I could have from a room full of adults.

Keep growing and asking questions. Be a lifelong learner, like I have heard so many inspirational people say. The more perspectives you hear, the better.

Sub-Lesson A: People come into your life for a reason. Listen and pay attention!

"When one door of happiness closes, another opens; but often we look so long at the closed door that we do not see the one which has been opened for us." – Helen Keller, *The Story of My Life*

Even though Alcoholics Anonymous was not for me, I will never forget one of the first conversations I had with a fellow recovering alcoholic. She shared her journey with me, of being an alcoholic until she had her children, becoming sober while they were growing up, only to turn back to alcohol after they grew into adults. This began to disintegrate her relationship with her children and grandchildren, and it took years of proof of her permanent sobriety until they could learn to trust her again. *This was a chilling realization for me that I can never drink again.* Romantic thoughts of "retiring" and drinking wine in Italy or sipping Mai Thais in Hawaii (what the hell is a Mai Thai even?) are no longer serving me. By hearing this from another person, I was able to avoid a similar disaster. And this is why I am so open about my sobriety, my mental health, and my traumas. Every bit of it is to help others so that they hopefully do not have to go through the same hell that I did.

Sub-Lesson B: Read more. You will learn so much about others AND yourself!

"One child, one teacher, one book, one pen can change the world." – Malala Yousafzai, *I Am Malala: The Story of the Girl Who Stood Up for Education and Was Shot by the Taliban*

I mean duh, right? As I read *The Body Keeps the Score* by the incredible Dr. Bessel Van Der Kolk, I had so many epiphanies as it related to my own childhood, the abuse that I endured, and how it affects my daily life now. The biggest one just may be that I *like* being angry, which is perhaps why I hold grudges. I love the way my blood boils when someone crosses me, or the way I blast Halsey's "Nightmare" or Cake's "Nugget" while I scream along with the lyrics. The more I think on it, the more I realize that this was a defense mechanism that I built growing up. If I was angry, I couldn't let the hurt get to me. Of course, every time I was physically or emotionally abused, it stung, but if I could just tense my whole body up and be PISSED, I would be OK. It was the way I *survived.* This is why I sought out ways to re-traumatize myself. I must have been subconsciously looking for something to upset me so that I could get mad. It's not a fun way to live, but it's the only way I knew. So it's up to me to change it. Fortunately for me, I have already engaged in some of the practices that Dr. Van Der Kolk mentions, such as yoga, meditation, and cognitive behavioral therapy. The reiki was also a way for me to separate myself from my scared lonely little girl and reconnect her to the adult Celeste so that she can now feel safe and be a whole part of me.

Reading more doesn't just mean books either, by the way. Read articles! And no, I don't mean the BuzzFeed articles that compare your personality to the cast of *Friends* (by the way, I'm Ross). I mean news articles, both fact and opinion, to challenge yourself constantly not only to know what the heck is going on in the world but also to learn from other people's perspectives. Especially in today's polarizing political atmosphere, it is more important than ever that we be open instead of closed-minded. I highly recommend supporting local journalism – not only will you glean information about what's going on in your community, but you can help support your neighbors!

One more place that I LOVE to get information from is podcasts (my editor is reminding me that this is not the same thing as reading, but sometimes when I listen to podcasts, I get just as much, if not more, information from them as I do books). I am also newly obsessed with audiobooks, going through them like water (I know you told me so, Trisha)! Find the topics and the themes that you love and/or want to know more about, and you will find that the time listening just flies by. It's such a great distraction while driving or doing chores around the house (or drowning your kids out, just saying).

Sub-Lesson C: Play nice with others, especially when they are on your team.

"I wonder about a world in which you can be kind to everyone but the people who belong to you." – Brittney Cooper, *Eloquent Rage*

I thought I was done with my book y'all, and then someone had to come along and hatefully repost my picture on Twitter with an angry condescending remark. It was a picture that I posted before our annual Moms Demand Action national conference, Gun Sense University. As I mentioned before, I knew that I would have haters, and I KNEW that they could come from within, but it somehow still surprised me and threw me for a loop. What I later found out from friends who have experienced the same hater-ade is that there are a group of women who used to be a part of Moms Demand Action who grew salty and decided to rebel against our movement by creating their own Twitter accounts under the pseudonym Betsy.

While I certainly empathize with the frustration that these women are feeling, the avenues that they have chosen to express their ire are disappointing. We are ALL fighting to end gun violence, so it would make sense that we all work TOGETHER, especially since our opposition is so well established (though it is finally crumbling, slowly but surely). We must really focus all of our energy on fighting for our righteous cause and not waste our anger on internal battles. Working together and linking arms makes us stronger, but it requires being open to different points of views and not getting caught up with egos and power struggles. **We must focus on lifting others UP, not tearing**

them down.

35

Life Lesson #18: Apologize if you say or do something stupid but don't apologize for just being.

"Whether life's disabilities left you outcast, bullied, or teased
　　Rejoice and love yourself today
　　'Cause, baby, you were born this way" Lady Gaga, in "Born This Way," by Paul Edward Blair, Fernando Garibay, Stefani J. Germanotta (Lady Gaga), and Jeppe Breum Laursen

I am pretty sure that we have already established that we all beat ourselves up more than anyone else, sometimes for no reason other than we just like tearing ourselves apart - or it has become a known value and a comfort to us. Imagine that – we are *comfortable* tearing ourselves down. *That shouldn't be a thing.*

　We constantly apologize for things that are completely out of our control or that are just human nature. If we get emotional while talking to someone, we apologize for crying. If we are walking down an aisle in the grocery store and happen to be right in front of something that another customer wants, we apologize instead of just saying excuse me (I do this every damn time). The worst example for me is when I know that I am right, but I just want to get along with the other person, so I apologize. All of these things are human nature. They are what we do while living our normal lives. We shouldn't have to apologize for them. We don't need to be sorry for crying, for inadvertently being in someone's way, or especially for being right!

I learned from my friend Mary Reed, who is an Everytown Survivor Fellow, as well as an American hero who shielded her daughter from bullets in Tucson during the Gaby Giffords shooting, that we should never apologize for crying when speaking of our grief. I have really taken this to heart. In fact, when I met my hero Senator Chris Murphy in Washington D.C., I unapologetically cried while telling him the story of my dad. As Mary points out, by me being so raw and real with him, he was able to empathize with me and catch a glimpse of what it's like to live in my shoes.

The same goes for our emotion and our tears at any other time. Ever since hearing Mary's powerful words, telling us to just let our tears flow, I cringe every time I see someone apologize for their tears or for expressing their feelings. While I know that vulnerability is hard, it is also natural to feel this way. To be human. To show emotion. To react to things in a real way. After all, we aren't robots! And in the words of Brené Brown, we aren't sociopaths either (at least I hope you aren't if you have made it this far into my book). **Real people with real feelings experience real emotions**, and it's absolutely OK to convey them. Stop apologizing, people! Let others react to your emotion. I promise you that you are in no way inconveniencing them by your tears.

Let's also think of other things we can say instead of "I'm sorry" all the time. Honestly, I get sick of myself saying it so much. I do enough dumb shit that I need to *for real* apologize for, so when it comes to the everyday stuff I am doing, like being in someone's way or not having exact change or any number of benign things my kids did that were out of my control, I think it's best to just be up front. We can just state the facts. "Oh, excuse me, I was getting the same item you are looking for." "I just have a $20. Do you have change for me?" "My sons are 8 and 10. They are learning." (Let me tell you, it really took a lot for me to come up with that last sentence because half the time I am convinced that my kids are assholes, so I do often feel that apologies are necessary!)

Listen, it's great that we all apologize. But if we use the term "I'm sorry" too much or in a generic way, doesn't it lose its meaning? I am constantly telling my eldest son Adam that I don't believe him or I am not yet ready to forgive him because he doles out "I'm sorry"s like candy. **We have to be very specific, intentional, and meaningful with our apologies.**

Let's not waste our apologies for nothing. After all, words are just words until we put them into action. I have certainly made many mistakes along the way, making opinionated comments to people I didn't know well, not realizing that the things I was insulting were things that they held dear. (I find myself putting my head in my hands as I am typing this, feeling so ashamed for my ignorance. However, each time I do something like this, it teaches me to be more careful in the future.)

Sub-Lesson A: Stop beating yourself up. Nothing is accomplished by this. You only make yourself feel worse.

"I'm so sick of running as fast I can
    Wondering if I'd get there quicker
    If I was a man" – Taylor Swift, in "The Man," by Taylor Swift and Joel Little

Speaking of feeling ashamed, can we just stop beating ourselves up for goodness sake about things that we think are "bad?" I just had this epiphany yesterday, when I woke up and spent yet another morning contemplating what I could eat that wouldn't consume too many calories because I am still feeling guilty for the amount of homemade peanut butter oatmeal chocolate chip cookies I devoured two days in row. My weight has been a constant point of contention in my life from the time I can remember. From being a chubby kid to incessantly hating myself as an adult for my love of sugar, the self-control that I maintain to work out virtually every day just isn't there when you put a gluten free cookie or ice cream in front of me (especially Ben & Jerry's Phish Food®, with which I was recently reacquainted and am obsessed). Like many people (or at least I tell myself), my taste buds crave sugar when I am finished with a meal. They crave that final touch of deliciousness for me to enjoy, which I then beat myself up over later. But what if I just accepted the fact that I love food? Instead of attacking myself, why can't I just love myself? What a freaking concept.

Another thing that has come to my attention lately is the

amount of self-loathing that has consumed me since I was a child for not being able to sit still or pay attention for significant amounts of time. It wasn't until reading a book on ADHD for my son that I suddenly realized I have had the condition my entire life. No wonder I am so hyperactive when I am excited and so prone to narcolepsy when I am bored or forced to sit for too long. Even while writing this book, I have to take multiple breaks. My life is a constant state of organized chaos, just the way I like it. Now that I understand myself better, I can redirect my energies and stop beating myself up for things that are not in my control. **Understanding yourself is key.**

36

Life Lesson #19: Thank people along the way, and give credit where credit is due.

"I don't wanna wear your crown, there's enough to go around."
- Maren Morris in "GIRL," by Greg Allen Kurstin, Maren Larae Morris, and Sarah Paige Aarons

While saying "I'm sorry" repeatedly can have a wearing effect, I don't think that we can say "thank you" enough to people who do nice things for us. Of course, you always hear people saying that "It's nothing," or "Please, don't thank me," but really, *how do we feel when our kind acts go unnoticed or unappreciated?* Pretty shitty, right? That's why the small act of saying thank you to people is so damn important. It's why thank you cards are so necessary. If we can give goody bags at all of our kids' parties, we can damn sure take the time to write a thank you card for the gifts that people were so generous to give our children (or even just a text, though I am old-fashioned and love the significance of the hand-written card).

Talented individuals deserve to be acknowledged. Every time I post pictures on my Instagram that my talented photographer friends took, I tag them and thank them. I may have posed for the picture, but I didn't set up the lighting or frame it perfectly. This is why companies trademark things. (If everyone were honest, we wouldn't have to do this. *Wouldn't that be nice?*)

There is so much gratification that comes from thanking people and giving credit where credit is due, or at least that is my experience. I love thanking people along the way and telling them that they inspired me and/or helped me to get to where I am currently. I am usually met with a thank you in return. Thanking each other is so powerful and generates a warmth inside of our bodies like nothing else.

Sub-Lesson A: Accept praise with gratitude.

"Life is not meant to be lived as a Lone Wolf. We all need a Pack."
– Abby Wambach, *Wolfpack*

When YOU receive credit or praise, it's extremely important to be able to accept it with grace and humility. Think about the meaning of the words that the other person is saying to you, and really take them to heart. They wouldn't be telling you how awesome you are, how hard you are working, or how delicious your food is if they didn't genuinely believe it. You have clearly made an impact on them by sharing your beautiful gifts, and here is your moment to let that appreciation sink in. Bask in it.

If you have a hard time accepting praise, there is likely some psychological reason for that, which I will admit that I am completely unqualified to dole out advice for, but I will tell you this – BELIEVE IN YOURSELF! You worked so hard to be who you are, to get to where you are, and **there is truly no one else like you**. Embrace that.

37

Life Lesson #20: It's not about getting credit. It's about doing what's decent and right for that reason only, not to receive recognition or praise.

"I would like to be remembered as a person who wanted to be free... so other people would be also free." – Rosa Parks, Source Unknown (I would really love to know where all of these brilliant quotes came from, as the Internet seems quite sure that these bold brave goddesses said them.)

I realize that this life lesson conflicts with the lesson before it but please hear me out. While it is so important for us to GIVE people credit, we should never BANK on it ourselves. We shouldn't do our good deeds just because we think that someone is going to say thank you or give us a shout out. This just makes us an addict for attention and praise.

Yes, we are all awesome and worthy of all the love and all the praise, BUT we mustn't let said praise and accomplishments get to our heads. This can lead us down a self-righteous, egotistical path. Not always, but it's certainly a dangerous slope on which to start. If we begin only doing things because we know that we will get credit for them, what does that say about our purpose in life? Personally, I wouldn't want to live that way – relying on others for self-assurances.

I used to crave the attention and the thanks from people. In fact, as I have watched celebrities on Instagram do their Lives, I think to myself that maybe I shouldn't even bother with mine because I am *lucky* if I get a few viewers on my Lives. My ego isn't being fed and it's fucking hungry. Then I remember that these celebrities worked hard to get to where they are to receive their many followers. Perhaps my day will come. In the meantime, I need to just let that shit go and tell my ego to chill out.

My friend Richard Martinez is famous for saying that nothing else that he did before his son was killed matters now. All that matters is the work he is doing to end gun violence in this country. He is concerned about the greater good. He doesn't do it for the praise or thanks (and believe me, he gets a lot because he is totally awesome); he does it because he knows that it's the right thing to do.

It's human nature to seek validation. As my former therapist told me, "We need to feel wanted and we want to feel needed." I think that we can accomplish this while letting go of our expectations of the outcome or the thanks that we may get. When I teach yoga, I do so to practice my own mindfulness and to help others tune into theirs as well. I feel needed and wanted while doing this, but I don't *expect* to receive praise for doing this service. This just makes it feel all the better when I actually do receive it. I really mean it when I tell people that they make my day with their kind words.

Sub-Lesson A: The little things matter more than you know.

"Each one of us matters, has a role to play, and makes a difference." – Jane Goodall, *Reason for Hope: A Spiritual Journey*

Jane Goodall, chimpanzee champion and nature ambassador, is also quoted as saying, "You cannot get through a single day without having an impact on the world around you." At the end of the day, I often relive each part. Sometimes I think through each task as I am doing it throughout the day, noting what impact it has in the world. From posting inspirational Lives on my social media, to recycling everything that I can, to instilling my own values in my children, I (theoretically) can rest each night knowing that I have contributed positively to the world around me. That said, it sure is difficult to turn on the news and watch the horrendous things happening around the world, feeling like there is so much out of my control. This is where I must focus on what I CAN do.

Things I can do:

1. Take care of myself so that I can take care of others
2. Tend to my children and their needs
3. Donate money or resources to charity
4. Check in on my friends through texts or phone calls
5. Send my family and friends gifts and/or cards
6. Limit the number of resources that I am using on this precious planet
7. Share my positivity with the world in person and on social

media

8. Continue to educate myself so that I can help educate others

Voila! I know that if I do all of this, I am doing what I can, and *that is enough.*

38

Life Lesson #21: Constantly remind yourself that you're awesome!!

"If you don't have something nice to say, don't say anything – this also applies to ourselves." - Jess Sims, *Peloton workout*

This can be so difficult. Many of us are quick to praise others, yet we are so hard on ourselves. We love to ruminate on how we could have done things differently, AKA better. My former therapist wisely recommended for me to treat myself like my own best friend. This immediately changed the way that I treated myself. Now, when I start to beat myself up, I stop and ask myself if I would treat my best friend this way. While it's a challenge, it has made such a positive impact on my life.

I once heard some advice on a podcast, where the guest stated that he puts positive reminders on his phone every day (and I've since learned that there are affirmation apps that do this for you too, so I now use the "I am" app and love it). I immediately implemented this advice, and it's been life changing. While I no longer get my 7 AM reminder that *I am crushing it at life* (because it was really fucking annoying before my coffee), I love my 4 PM reminder to *take a deep breath*, and no matter how much I believe it or not, to read every night at 8 PM that *I am a great mom* is sure a beautiful thing.

Another thing I once did was recommended by an incredible holistic health coach friend of mine. I took mini–Post-it Notes and wrote a positive word on each one to put up above my desk. I knew I needed the encouragement, and it worked. Each word represented one of my strengths. Each one reminded me of my purpose. Most of all, each one spoke to me when I was having an anxious or depressed day, telling me that I am truly worthy whether my brain currently felt that way or not.

Sub-Lesson A: Stop telling yourself the lie that you can't.

"We all know the inequalities that women have faced, and that for centuries there was opposition to women being heard. We all know that cultural norms and social conditioning cause some women to impose limitations on themselves and be overly self-critical." – Viv Groskop, *How to Own the Room: Women and the Art of Brilliant Speaking*

Ugh, this is the worst. You know you have to do something, and your brain starts firing messages to you that you aren't capable even though you know in your veins that you most certainly are. It happens to me on a regular basis. From running to yoga to creating a PowerPoint presentation, my procrastinating brain silently smiles its sinister smile, repeating this BS over and over until I just finally fucking DO the thing. And then, boom! I proved it wrong. The cycle repeats itself next time I hop on the treadmill or boot up my computer. It's exhausting.

This is where I have to tap into my warrior mindset, my confidence and self-compassion, so that I can stop feeling so inadequate. While these feelings are all too common, we must work to make them less so. We must be our own biggest cheerleaders. **If we can't cheer for ourselves, how the hell can we expect anyone else to cheer for us?**

Sub-Lesson B: Note when you make progress and celebrate it!

"Say it loud and proud! Good work isn't enough; we need to promote, promote, promote. No, it's not bragging. It's the truth. Speak your truth to as many people as will listen!" – Erin Vilardi, " Erin Vilardi Helps Diverse Women Unleash Their Political Power To Transform American Democracy," *LadyBossBlogger*

Sometimes it is easier to set small goals and accomplish a little at a time, as opposed to having one big target. I have found that when I have a daunting project that I am procrastinating over (ahem, this book perhaps?), if I decide that I am going to accomplish a little bit each day, it is much easier to do than trying to set aside a block of hours (which, let's face it – who has that kind of time in their schedule if you have kids, especially during a pandemic?). By deciding that I am merely going to write for 15 minutes a day, I accomplish a hell of a lot more than if I were writing for 2 hours every 2 months. **Tasks are much easier accomplished with smaller, more attainable goals.** James Clear, author of *Atomic Habits*, shares how to do this is his book. He states that even by showing up every day to the gym, without working out, we are training our mind to make it a part of our routine. He recommends starting small – way smaller than you think – and eventually you can build to those larger, more fulfilling goals.

My husband has also introduced me to the Pomodoro technique, where you work for a certain period of time, then take a small break, then work again, followed by another break. This can help maintain your focus, especially if you have ADHD like me. Then, on my breaks, I get to do fun things!

Instead of waiting until you have finished a book or earned an award or finished whatever incredible thing you are into, celebrate the small wins! Who's to say you have to wait until the end of your project to do a happy dance? **It's so easy to get burned out if we make ourselves go until we collapse.** (I suggest re-reading Life Lesson #9 right now if you have a habit of this.) Break out that happy music and start celebrating, you fabulous person you!!

39

Life Lesson #22: Listen to your own advice!

"I am always writing what I need to hear and teaching what I need to learn." – Glennon Doyle, *We Can Do Hard Things* Podcast

After writing all of the above life lessons to help others, this one is for myself. Isn't it easier to be kinder to others than it is to ourselves? We must take the beautiful words that we tell others when trying to encourage them, validate them, or lift them up, and apply them to ourselves.

Be kind and gentle to yourself.

Sometimes it just helps to sit in your own feelings. Feelings suck. Am I right? One day while sitting with my Dharma Recovery peeps, we were discussing being alone with ourselves and how difficult it can be to just acknowledge our feelings. So many people stay busy so that they don't have time to reflect on who they are and what they are feeling. If you are someone who has led a complicated life, it can be incredibly painful to practice this. It is so much easier to numb yourself, which is exactly what I did with alcohol for so many years. As time goes by, the pain gets easier to tolerate, but there are still days when it rises up from my belly and I feel as if I could breathe fire. The anger is there; it's palpable. What matters is what I do with it.

You will know when you've found your passion.

Nothing can stop you.

You will not lose your voice.

Your body will naturally show you the way.

You have the motivation and the strength.

You don't need anyone to push you.

You got this!

Now, go be a bold brave goddess!

www.ingramcontent.com/pod-product-compliance
Lightning Source LLC
Chambersburg PA
CBHW060155130626
46556CB00006B/2651